the terry lectures
THINKING IN CIRCLES

MARY DOUGLAS

Thinking in Circles

An Essay on Ring Composition

YALE UNIVERSITY PRESS · NEW HAVEN AND LONDON

Printed in the United States of America.

Library of Congress Cataloging-in-Publication Data
Douglas, Mary, 1921–
Thinking in circles : an essay on ring composition / Mary
Douglas.
p. cm. — (The Terry lectures)
Includes bibliographical references and index.
ISBN-13: 978-0-300-11762-2 (cloth : alk. paper)
ISBN-10: 0-300-11762-0
1. Narration (Rhetoric) 2. Homer, Iliad. 3. Bible. O.T.
Numbers — Criticism, interpretation, etc. 4. Sterne,
Laurence, 1713–1768. Life and opinions of Tristram
Shandy, gentleman. I. Title.
PN212.D68 2007
808 — dc22
2006020410

A catalogue record for this book is available from the
British Library.

The paper in this book meets the guidelines for perma-
nence and durability of the Committee on Production
Guidelines for Book Longevity of the Council on Library
Resources.

10 9 8 7 6 5 4 3 2 1

THE DWIGHT HARRINGTON TERRY
FOUNDATION LECTURES ON
RELIGION IN THE
LIGHT OF SCIENCE AND PHILOSOPHY

The deed of gift declares that "the object of this foundation is not the promotion of scientific investigation and discovery, but rather the assimilation and interpretation of that which has been or shall be hereafter discovered, and its application to human welfare, especially by the building of the truths of science and philosophy into the structure of a broadened and purified religion. The founder believes that such a religion will greatly stimulate intelligent effort for the improvement of human conditions and the advancement of the race in strength and excellence of character. To this end it is desired that a series of lectures be given by men eminent in their respective departments, on ethics, the history of civilization and religion, biblical research, all sciences and branches of knowledge which have an important bearing on the subject, all the great laws of nature, especially of evolution . . . also such interpretations of literature and sociology as are in accord with the spirit of this foundation, to the end that the Christian spirit may be nurtured in the fullest light of the world's knowledge and that mankind may be helped to attain its highest possible welfare and happiness upon this earth." The present work constitutes the latest volume published on this foundation.

CONTENTS

CONTENTS IN A RING

PREFACE

To publish at last an essay on ring composition is a great personal satisfaction. I first read the book of Numbers in 1987 and was surprised to find that it has been much depreciated by commentators for disorderly writing. I later found that it is not disorderly but well organized as an elegant ring.

After seeing how badly that great book has fared at the hands of qualified commentators, I could not get the topic off my mind. I was, and still am, convinced that there is a lot that ought to be better known about ring composition. Something should be done to end the unworthy slurs on great authors and ancient texts. I put off making a serious study because I was not nearly qualified (and I still am not). The topic is arcane; the ground has been dug over many times by specialist scholars commanding many languages. I must regard myself as a visitor to the field of biblical scholarship. To have the courage to make a strong complaint I would have had to focus on the task exclusively and put everything else aside for at least a decade. Given these obstacles, I would never have made a start but for the honor of an invitation from King's College London in 2002 to give the F. D. Maurice Lectures. There was absolutely no restriction on topic, and no requirement to publish. Instead of the profound and scholarly review that the occasion deserved, I settled for just waving a flag. I wanted to make the lectures a call for help. In effect, help was given so generously that when I had a second invitation from Yale University to give the Terry Lectures the next year my diffidence had been dispelled.

The audience at King's College had been stimulating and almost too polite. I jumped at the chance to invite more criticism and discussion. The audience at Yale was just as polite and full of stimulating suggestions, most of which I have tried to follow in these pages. I remember gratefully discussions with Geoffrey Hartman and David

Apter, and the strong support of Dianne Witte, who organized everything. By the time I had finished I realized that the project was even
more formidable than I had originally feared. I am grateful that Yale
University Press offered to publish the second set of lectures on ring
composition.

Ring composition is found all over the world, not just in a few
places stemming from the Middle East, so it is a worldwide method of
writing. It is a construction of parallelisms that must open a theme,
develop it, and round it off by bringing the conclusion back to the
beginning. It sounds simple, but, paradoxically, ring composition is
extremely difficult for Westerners to recognize. To me this is myste-
rious. Apparently, when Western scholars perceive the texts to be
muddled and class the authors as simpletons, it is because they do not
recognize the unfamiliar method of construction.

Friends ask me, what does it matter? Why is it important to know
the construction? This leads to another point: in a ring composition
the meaning is located in the middle. A reader who reads a ring as if
it were a straight linear composition will miss the meaning. Surely
that matters! The text is seriously misunderstood, the composition is
classed as lacking in syntax, and the author dismissed with disdain.
Surely, misinterpretation does matter.

The anthropologists' standard criticism of attempts to interpret
mythology apply to this venture. A typical gibe is to accuse the would-
be myth analyst of giving free rein to her imagination. Friends have
said, "Ring composition is a loose and fuzzy concept, Mary will always be able to find a ring form if she looks hard enough, in a laundry
list, sports news, or whatever. Rings are everywhere." This lethal
criticism I must rebut. Fear of it was one of the reasons why I was not
too disappointed to find that Leviticus is not an example of construction in a ring.

I had very much hoped to reveal the ring form of that book; I tried
hard and I failed. The consolation was to discover that Leviticus
conformed to another famous type of composition, figure poetry,
which I was not expecting at all. So the method of enquiry was justified even though the results, as far as ring composition is concerned,

were negative. Healthy respect for the same criticism from Bible scholars accounts for my interest in identifying the rules that the ring authors have been following, and accounts also for some rather heavy treatment.

The chapters in this volume start with describing and analyzing ring compositions so that the reader has the tools for discovering them, and for appreciating the causes of misreading. Antique ring compositions are a precious heritage. There exist many more than I have described, all liable to the rejection that I have noted. It is necessary to work out what the maligned authors were originally saying. If it is only to rehabilitate them the task is worthy.

I have tried to sum up a few compositional rules, but I know they only apply to certain types of ring composition. If any two students were put in non-communicating rooms, each furnished with a set of these seven rules and a copy of a given ring document, I hope they would come out agreeing on the pattern they had found in it. It is an experiment that I admit I have never had the chance to try.

Pursuing this topic I discovered many new friends. In 1989 I had the temerity to lecture on the book of Numbers. That year the Gifford Lectures were held in Edinburgh in the Divinity School, and I had the good fortune to have a chivalrous Bible scholar, Graeme Auld, as my host. He is an indefatigable pattern spotter; from his analyses of one biblical story plotted upon another story from another Bible book, he has forged a powerful exegetical tool for challenging received ideas about the history and order of the biblical texts. It is thanks to his learned example and his personal support that I have gone on adventuring among ring compositions.

We need to reread them systematically with a view to making a typology of the different kinds of rings, the places and periods they flourished in. In this thought I have been inspired by the late Yehuda Radday, who did so much of the basic work on biblical chiasmus. He told me (in private correspondence) that he hoped that a typological comparison of ring styles would be useful background for the controversies on dating of Bible writings, a hope I share.

When I was at Northwestern University I had the privilege of hearing Wolfgang Roth's lecture on the pattern of the miracles in Mark's gospel. It made me remember and never again forget that pattern perception is one of the basic skills of anthropology. At that time I had not started to work on the anthropology of the Bible. Back in London after 1988, I gratefully acknowledge encouragement from Mark Geller, head of the Institute of Jewish Studies in University College. Directly on the topic of ring composition, by a stroke of good luck I met Simon Weightman, of the School of Oriental and African Studies. He himself was working with Aditya Behl on early Persian poetry, both experienced in formal analysis. I have referred to their exciting studies in this volume. And for invaluable help on figured poetry (or picture poems) I am immensely grateful to Jeremy Adler.

Most of the friends who helped me with this book are colleagues of long standing whose help is too pervasive to be picked out for this specialized topic — for example, Wendy Doniger, who has talked about it with me several times. But some are friendships made specifically on account of research into ring composition. Joan Pittock, for example, I met by sheer luck, when I visited the University of Aberdeen for a conference on the Bible. She is researching in eighteenth-century literature, focusing particularly on the history of the Oxford Chair of Poetry. She introduced me to the background of Robert Lowth's famous lectures on Hebrew poetry, whose influence on the study of biblical literary styles, including ring composition, cannot be overestimated. Again it was by luck that I first met my friend, Milena Dolezelova, the Czech sinologist, also very interested in chiastic structures. She it was who introduced me to Chinese literary conventions, including novels composed as rings. Geoffrey Lloyd also helped me by suggesting that I should think of Chinese divination in connection with parallelism.

I am indebted to Alan Griffiths, Leonard Muellner, and Malcolm Willcock for valuable advice on the chapters on the *Iliad*. My biggest debt is to Simon Hornblower, who was, when we met at UCL in 1997, researching on ring composition in Herodotus and Thucydides. He introduced me to John Myres's account of "pedimental" writing. "Pedimental" means writing that goes up to a central point, makes a turn, then comes down step by step on the other side, like wide-angled pediments on doorways. "Pedimental," as another name for a chiasmus, is usually applied to short pieces of writing, whereas I am using the words "ring composition" for much longer texts. It is like the difference between the decoration on a porch and the structure of the house.

The idea of a pedimental composition is clearly seen in Jacob Milgrom's design of a biblical ring that embraces in its scope the whole of the Pentateuch and the Book of Joshua. He has drawn a steeply angled mountain labeled "The Theological-Literary Structure of the Hexateuch" (Fig. 1). The left side, ascending from Genesis, is labeled with an arrow "From Slavery"; on the peak, referring to Exodus, is "Theophany, My Presence." Coming down from the top on the right-hand side the arrow points "To Freedom," referring to Leviticus, Numbers, Deuteronomy, and Joshua (four books are rolling down the mountainside much more quickly than the first two climbed up).

The ring is closed by the reference at the end to "Land promise fulfilled," Joshua (13–24), which matches "Land promised" at the beginning (Genesis 12–50). It shows how the circle does what writing in rings can do: raise the level of understanding.

It is a pleasure to record my debt in this book to Jacob Milgrom, specially for help on the chapters on Numbers. Without his learned support sustained over twenty years I never would have persevered with the study of the Bible as literature.

Ending is different from completion, as I have explained in the last chapter; the first is difficult, and the second impossible. I thank these people for their inestimable help. It is such a pleasure to remember them that I could go on for pages, as there are many more debts to acknowledge.

I would not forget to thank my sister, Pat Novy, for her line drawings of Abraham and Isaac, for the drawing of the scroll whose meaning is in the middle, and for her ring diagrams that vindicate such disparate materials being brought together under the one head of "Ring Composition." I also thank Tom Fardon for taking time off

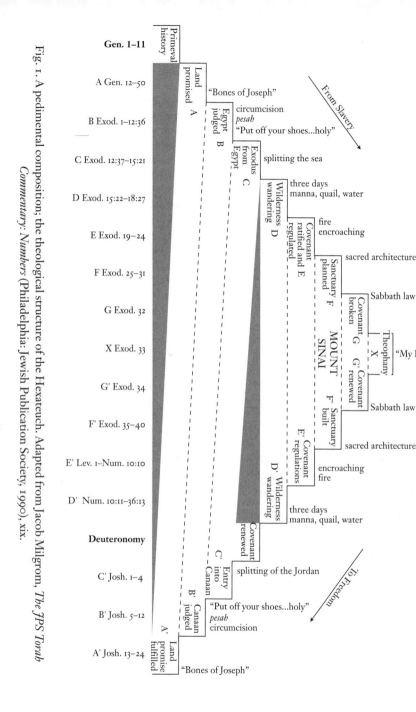

Fig. 1. A pedimental composition; the theological structure of the Hexateuch. Adapted from Jacob Milgrom, *The JPS Torah Commentary: Numbers* (Philadelphia: Jewish Publication Society, 1990), xix.

Gen. 1–11   Primeval history

A Gen. 12–50   Land promised A   "Bones of Joseph"

B Exod. 1–12:36   Egypt judged B   circumcision / *pesaḥ* / "Put off your shoes...holy"

C Exod. 12:37–15:21   Exodus from Egypt C   splitting the sea

D Exod. 15:22–18:27   Wilderness wandering D   three days / manna, quail, water

E Exod. 19–24   Covenant ratified and regulated E   fire encroaching

F Exod. 25–31   Sanctuary planned F   sacred architecture

G Exod. 32   Covenant broken G   Sabbath law

X Exod. 33   Theophany X   "My Presence"

G' Exod. 34   G' Covenant renewed   Sabbath law

F' Exod. 35–40   F' Sanctuary built   sacred architecture

E' Lev. 1–Num. 10:10   E' Covenant regulations   encroaching fire

D' Num. 10:11–36:13   D' Wilderness wandering   three days / manna, quail, water

Deuteronomy   Covenant renewed

C' Josh. 1–4   C' Entry into Canaan   splitting of the Jordan

B' Josh. 5–12   B' Canaan judged   "Put off your shoes...holy" / *pesaḥ* / circumcision

A' Josh. 13–24   A' Land promise fulfilled   "Bones of Joseph"

MOUNT SINAI

From Slavery

To Freedom

from his school leaving examinations and for giving invaluable skill in the tricky work of preparing the typescript for the publishers. I also extend thanks to my friendly neighbor, Colin Donne, for computer diagrams. Of course I gratefully acknowledge the publishers themselves, notably Jean Black and her team, Laura Davulis for her patience in the work of turning this typescript into a book, and Joyce Ippolito for her extreme care and attention to the text.

A new interest in ring composition has lately arisen. This antique literary form is being discovered in documents that the scholars have known for centuries and have translated without recognizing that they have any formal structure. Many fine old texts have been disdained and disrespectfully mauled in the effort to get to the sense. What a shame, and what dull and trivial interpretations have been piously accepted in default! And how ready the commentators were to lay the perceived incoherences to the door of weak writing skills, or even weak intelligence. Writings that used to baffle and dismay unprepared readers, when read correctly, turn out to be marvelously controlled and complex compositions. Learning how they were constructed is like a revelation, with something of the excitement of hidden treasure. Now is a good moment for the effort of rereading. Various disciplines are taking up the task.

Glenn Most has pointed out a paradox in the reading of Pindar. In antiquity no one thought his poetry was particularly "difficult," but in modern times he is seen as "the very paradigm of poetic difficulty . . . an esoteric poet in whom clarity of thought . . . is mantled over by so thorough an obscurity of expression that the meaning of individual phrases is already often impenetrable and the organization of poems as wholes scarcely imaginable."[1] The stories of misreadings that I could tell are nearly as shocking.

The minimum criterion for a ring composition is for the ending to join up with the beginning. Chapter 2 gives more detail. A ring is a framing device. The linking up of starting point and end creates an envelope that contains everything between the opening phrases and the conclusion. The rule for closing the ring endows the work with unity; it also causes all the problems that another set of rules has been designed to solve. It takes skill to compose a polished specimen. There has to be a well-marked point at which the ring turns, preparatory to working back to the beginning, and the whole series of stanzas from the beginning to the middle should be in parallel with the other series going from the middle back to the start. Each section on the second side of the ring corresponds to a matching section on the first side. The form is well known. It is basically the chiastic structure, ABBA, or ABCBA, a form that pervades the Bible and other famous archaic texts. It comes in many sizes, from a few lines to a whole book enclosed in its macro-envelope, arranged throughout in intricately corresponding parallelisms.[2] It is called either *inclusio*, emphasizing the bracketing into one unit of everything from the start to the end, or *chiasmus*, emphasizing the inverted word order.

Jacob Milgrom takes a fine example of phrase inversion from the Book of Numbers.[3] On the march of the Israelites to the Jordan, two tribes see land where they would like to settle. They ask Moses, but he refuses to let them take any land for themselves until the whole journey is accomplished; he requires the warriors of Israel to fight side by side all the way to the final victory. First they ask Moses, saying:

A   We will build here sheepfolds for our flocks
B   and cities for our little ones. (Num. 32.16)

He expostulates, but when they promise to stay fighting with their comrades until victory, he concedes their wishes, reverting to their own words, but in reversed order.

B'   Build cities for your little ones
A'   And sheepfolds for your flocks. (Num. 32.24)

These are very short examples. What I mainly have in mind when I refer to ring composition is the large-scale, blown-up version of the same structure. A single ring is inclusive enough to comprise the whole of the book of Numbers; other rings include equally eminent and even lengthier texts. The small version can depend on repeated key word clusters for recognizing the structure. The macro-composition has to organize whole verses and paragraphs first in one ordering and then again in reverse order. This form is readily appreciated and understood by scholars when it includes only a few sentences. The large compositions constructed in this way, however, have had a bad reception in the West. The ring form has had a history of misunderstanding and disregard.

Holding the Oxford Chair of Poetry, Bishop Robert Lowth gave thirty-four lectures in Latin on the sacred poetry of the Bible.[4] He distinguished four types of Hebrew parallelism, and named the following varieties:

Synonymous parallelism: poems chanted by two groups, repeating back and forth:

When Israel went out of Egypt
The house of Jacob from a strange people. [Psalm 116]
AB/A'B'

(The words are not the same, but they are synonymous: Jacob's other name was Israel, Egypt was indeed a strange people to Israel.)

A   If only we had died
B   in the land of Egypt.
B'   or in this wilderness
A'   If only we had died. (Num. 14.2)

Antithetic parallelism: an image illustrated by its contrary, in the same exactly repeated pattern, but sentiments opposed to sentiments, words to words, singulars to singulars, plurals to plurals.
Example from Proverbs 27.6–7:

The blows of a friend are faithful, but the kisses of an enemy are
    treacherous.
The cloyed will trample on a honeycomb, but to the hungry every
    bitter thing is sweet.

Synthetic or constructive parallelism: the parallel lies only in the construction, for example, using numbers, triplets, and detailed balancing of syllable with syllable.

Example from Deuteronomy 32.2:

My doctrine shall drop, as the rain.
My word shall distill as the dew.

Or antithetic and synthetic parallelism can be combined.

Example from Isaiah 9:

> The bricks are fallen, but we will rebuild them with stone.
> The sycamores are cut down, but we will replace them with cedars.
> ABC B′ A″.

Bible scholars do not use Lowth's terminology nowadays, but they do write about parallelism, introverted parallelism, and chiasmus or chiastic structure, in which a pair of items reverses itself, yielding the pattern ABB′A′. Milgrom calls it "chiasm in subsequent repetition."[5]

After Lowth had spoken, a tacit presumption grew up to the effect that chiastic structures are essentially part of the Semitic literary heritage. They were not explicitly assimilated to ring composition in the Greek classics until W. A. A. van Otterlo's systematic study of ring composition in Homer. There was soon as much to say about Greek ring form as about Semitic chiasmus. The two fields, biblical and classical, continued on their separate ways, which was very reasonable as each had to do with evolved and regionally distinct literary conventions, each having its own history. Different or additional terms were used by Greek scholars; paratactic contrasted with syntactic, the parallelism with the punch at the end is called "priamel." For a biblical example:

> Saul has smote his thousands,
> And David his ten thousands. (1 Sam. 18.7)

Saul was very angry when he heard the women singing this.

The problems and the need for specialized terms arise when we discover that this literary form is not confined to two cultural regions but is universally present in archaic literary forms as well as in contemporary folkloric recitals. Roman Jakobson, the great philologist, surveyed the forms of parallelism among the peoples of the Ural-Atlantic area, where Finnish oral poetry offers the classic case. He said he was astonished to realize that the strong presence of parallelism "seemed hardly to interest the specialists in Russian folklore."[6] Following in his footsteps, the anthropologist James Fox has collected further evidence of it in major collections of texts from the Austronesian peoples, central Rotinese, the Celebes, the islands of eastern Indonesia.[7] Parallelism appears in millennia-old Chinese poetry and in the ancient Hawaiian creation chants. Speakers of Papuan languages in Timor and New Guinea use it. Parallelism remains dominant in Chinese literature, it is a common literary form in Borneo and Madagascar and in Vietnamese parallel poetry, and similar traditions exist among the Burmese and Thai.

Roman Jakobson described parallelism broadly as "a system of steady correspondences in composition and order of elements on many different levels: syntactic constructions, grammatical forms and grammatical categories, lexical synonyms and total lexical identities, and finally combinations of sounds and prosodic schemes. This system confers upon the lines connected through parallelism both clear uniformity and great diversity. Against the background of the integral matrix, the effect of the variations of phonic, grammatical, and lexical forms and meanings appears particularly eloquent."[8]

In the same chapter Jakobson quoted with approval Gerard Manley Hopkins saying in 1865: "The artificial part of poetry, perhaps we shall be right to say all artifice, reduces itself to the principle of parallelism."[9] For his own example of parallelism Roman Jakobson chose Edgar Allan Poe's lines:

To One in Paradise:
And all my days are trances,
And all my nightly dreams
Are where thy dark eye glances
And where thy footstep gleams.[10]

In these lines, day and night are complementary, and so are eye and foot, and dark and gleaming. There are some delicate transpositions when darkness is attributed to the dancer's eye, and the gleaming to her foot (presumably she has jewels on her toes). These poetic examples are pleasing parallels; they are not rings. There is no crossing over halfway through the series and no matching of the beginning with the ending, no ring form.

Ring composition is parallelism with an important difference. It is based on parallelism in the straightforward sense that one section has to be read in connection with another that is parallel because it covers similar or antithetical situations, and some of the same vocabulary acts as cues to the pairing. But the parallel sections are not juxtaposed in the texts. They must be placed opposite each other, one on each side of the ring. The structure is chiastic; it depends on the "crossing over" or change of direction of the movement at the middle point. A ring is much more interesting than a succession of simple parallels that are simply laid out consecutively. If ring composition were just a local literary form, like the sonnet adopted as a favored convention, or like a genre used for particular kinds of expression, elegiac, comic, or tragic, there would not be any big puzzle. Jakobson has launched a challenge by describing thinking in parallelisms as a faculty inherent in the relation among language, grammar, and the brain. If this is so, it would explain why the literary form based on it is so widespread. We should expect it to rise up anywhere, at any time, and it does, with many variants.

The local variations should not disguise the fact that the ring form appears to be extraordinarily stable over time. That should count as a point supporting Jakobson's theory about parallelism, by giving evidence that the same formal structure governs very ancient compositions. Zoroastrian literature includes seventeen poems (collectively known as the Gathas) that are attributed to Zoroaster himself.[11] They are found to correspond in their formal structure with other better known compositions, such as the *Iliad* and the book of Numbers, dating probably from between the eighth to the sixth centuries BCE. Greater antiquity is indicated by the forms the Gathas have in common with the Rig Veda. Sections of the composition are ordered in parallel stanzas, laid out in a single sequence until at a well-marked midpoint the sequence stops, turns around, and reversing the order of the stanzas returns the way it came, making an inverted parallel with the first sequence. So the simple chiastic pattern sustained through the centuries is AB C BA.

It is thanks to the relatively recent analyses of Martin Schwartz (who thoroughly systematized and greatly elaborated Hanns-Peter

Table 1. Zoroastrian hymns or gathas from the thirteenth
to the tenth centuries BCE.

(I a)	(I b)	(I c)
1 — 11	1 — 11	1 — 12
2 — 10	2 — 10	2 — 11
3 — 9	3 — 9	3 — 10
4 — 8	4 — 8	4 — 9
\5 — 7/	\5 — 7/	5 — 8
\6/	\6/	6 — 7

Schmidt's seminal observations of elements of ring composition in the Gathas of Zoroaster (Zarathushtra) that we can now appreciate the great technical complexity of the ring structures of this ancient poetry.[12] Verbal markers based on line and syllable count make links not only at line endings but systematically through all the stanzas of a composition.

Verses are put into correspondence with one another, echoing words and themes like rhyming structures in poetry, exploiting double meanings and puns. More complex patterns draw attention to the mid-turn stanza by nesting it in a threefold or even fourfold chiasmus of its own. Even more complex patterns link poems with each other in the same way, so that the poems once regarded as separate units can now be read as connected sequences. In 2003 Martin Schwartz recalled: "By about a decade ago I realized that in every Gathic poem *all* the stanzas are concatenated concentrically in accord with one of several patterns of symmetry, and that for each poem the central stanza(s), which are thematically significant, concatenate(s) with the immediately preceding and following stanzas, and, more importantly, with the first and last stanza."[13] In these words he has named the three basic principles of ring composition. Of these, the most important is the loading of the main message onto the central stanzas. Evidently in this literary convention, the interest lies in the elaborate word play. The semantic content of the poems seems limited and simple by contrast. In that period technical virtuosity counted for much more.

We can go even further back in time to discover ancient Chinese forms of parallelism.[14] In China in the eleventh millennium before Christ a form of divination was practiced that involved reading from marks on the shell of a tortoise (or turtle, either word).[15] Parallelism has always been prominent in Chinese poetry, philosophy, and literature.[16] Vandermeersch relates the dominance of parallelism in Chinese thought to the great importance of tortoise divination from early times.[17] Later it came to be absorbed into the cosmological pattern of the Yin and the Yang, which allocates every matter and its paired opposite into a philosophical dichotomy. The tortoise is taken to be a natural symbol of the cosmos; its carapace is round like heaven, underneath it is flat like the earth. The tortoise's extreme longevity puts it apart from other creatures. It has strongly marked right and left sides (Fig. 2).

The five horizontal lines represent the five elements: water, iron, earth, fire, and wood.[18] The diviners have systematically divided up five areas of the whole shell: the head end, the tail end, and three areas between the head and tail on each side, each with its own cosmic meanings. The diviners scorch the underside of the shell with a red-hot poker, making the surface crackle. During a consultation they would scrutinize the patterns of crackle marks on the shell with two written statements set up as binary contradiction. Crackles on the right side of the tortoise shell were read as positive responses, those on the left side as negative, in relation to the written statements. The patterns affirm or deny. It is sometimes a divination of a future event, sometimes a statement about the past or about the moral law, always highly technical and systematic, enjoying very great prestige.

The medieval Chinese novel was commonly dismissed by Chinese critics for lack of structure. To those unfamiliar with the tradition, a long story about highwaymen killing and plundering gave the impression of being the same story monotonously repeated over and over again. Hua I. Wu says: "many modern readers are disappointed and even annoyed by such repetitions and apparent clumsiness and until very recently the prevalent opinion was that *The Water Margins* and novels like it are episodic and lacking a coherent construction."[19]

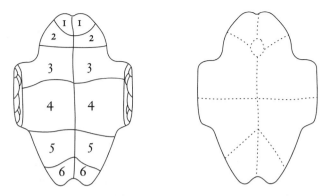

Fig. 2. Ancient Chinese divination on the tortoise shell.
Adapted from Léon Vandermeersch, "Les origines divinatoires
de la tradition chinoise du parallélisme littéraire," *Extrême-
Orient-Extrême-Occident* 11 (1989): 25.

"Repetition," "clumsiness," "episodic"! The complaint of incoherence will soon begin to sound familiar to my readers. In the seventeenth century the construction of the Chinese novel was revealed; it turns out to be based on elaborately entwined parallelisms. So the previous negative opinion was revised.

A fine survey of pre-modern Chinese literature summarizes its very old tradition of literary theory, starting in the thirteenth century in the form of theoretical prefaces to plays and novels, much influenced by an even older traditional theory of art, painting, and music.[20] The theory of literature seems to have developed in the seventeenth century as an important genre. It generated canons of poetry and elegant writing and instigated intense debates on the relation of art to morals and politics. Jin Shentang, a well-known dramatist and critic of the time, particularly emphasized parallelism as a structuring principle. He and his colleagues developed the thesis "that the novel is a finely constructed whole . . . a structure made up of components—themes, episodes, characters, sentences, words—that mutually resonate on both the syntagmatic and the paradigmatic levels of the text, endowing it with rhythmic dynamism and dramatic tension. The novel is thus a highly complex organization of a stratified character with multiple relationships whose patterns are set up at the text's beginning by a small unit (for example, a prologue or the first chapter) that is repeated, with textual variations, in larger units throughout the whole text."[21] This is well worth quoting because it anticipates what I want to say about ring composition in general, and in particular about the concept of repletion that I develop in Chapter 10.

There are many instances of misunderstanding, of a scholar despising or rejecting an antique text because of its alleged lack of order and syntax. In this volume I quote several examples of negative judgments made by learned commentators on ancient texts. The various cases of error are either due to the critic having missed altogether the internal structure of alternating parallels or due to their having missed the central place where the keys to the main theme are gathered together.

The Literary Guide to the Bible is a sophisticated book and a great achievement on practically every level.[22] But it is a pity that only a few of the contributors to a book with this title are interested in the Bible's dominant literary construction, parallelism. In a very fine chapter at its end, on "The Characteristics of Ancient Hebrew Poetry," Robert Alter makes a close analysis of parallelism in parts of particular poems, sometimes the psalms, and also short poetic structures, as from the book of Job or Samuel. Joel Rosenberg's impressive analysis of the prophets Jeremiah and Ezekiel is another exception.[23] He deploys the symmetries and parallels of the prophetic discourses to reveal the meanings of famously puzzling texts. He even summarizes the formal pattern of the whole book of Jeremiah in a clear chiastic structure. I am not able to judge the soundness of the analysis, but I regard the attempt as a major step toward replacing our own with contemporary literary judgments. Most of the other chapters apply modern literary standards, focusing on plots, themes, and personalities. They rarely show interest in the macro-structure of a long text. When they do say something about parallelism it is concerned with very short pieces, a few lines.

As I see it, the tracing of the total scheme from beginning to end and the concern for a coherent pattern would correspond to the biblical authors' own preoccupations, and implicitly to their criteria of literary excellence. I am particularly glad to read Rosenberg's remarks on earlier commentators who have found the texts elusive: "The Structure of Jeremiah, and especially of its apparently chaotic chronology, has proved elusive to critical investigators, many of whom have declared the text to be in disarray and have attempted a reconstruction of an 'original.' "[24] The terms *disarray* and *chaotic*, together with *disordered*, *clumsy*, and other pejoratives, will crop up very often as we proceed.

To show that these negative judgments on structure are not solely due to a blind spot in Western literary criticism, I quote the Persians' comments on the structure of the *chef d'oeuvre* of their own great mystic, Rumi. Simon Weightman has recently described the scholarly reception of Rumi's masterpiece, the *Mathnawi*.[25] The response to this famous mystical writing exactly echoes the response of certain biblical commentaries—for example, Martin Noth's misreading of the book of Numbers. Rumi's book is renowned, the commentators revere it, but they find fault with the author for failing "to keep the discourse on orderly lines." They complain that it consists of unconnected anecdotes, it is disjointed, and it is full of long digressions. Weightman mentions it being called "rambling," "a trackless ocean," lacking in "any firm framework." But in the case of religious mysticism, to discount the structure is not a criticism, and these remarks are not meant to be disparaging. On the contrary, the disorderly style, as the critics take it to be, is all the more esteemed because it is supposed to indicate a spontaneous flow of inspiration.

Whenever I read criticism of dire editorial confusion, my pulse quickens; I scent a hidden structure, probably a ring composition. In the case of Rumi's *Mathnawi* my gut response is vindicated. A doctoral student at the School of Oriental and African Studies, Seyed Ghahreman Savi-Homani, has closely examined the structure of Rumi's text. He demonstrates that it is not at all disorderly. It obeys very precisely the rules of a well-conceived and well-executed ring composition as I describe them in the next chapter.[26]

Why is ring composition practiced all over the world? What is it for? So many people! So many epochs! They could not have all learned it from one another. Its robustness over thousands of years supports the theory that something in the brain preserves it, and yet we know that it can fade out so completely that new readers miss it altogether.

Among speculations about the origin of this complicated rhetorical system, a common one is that it comes from pre-literate times where it was a necessary help to the memory of the bards. It is true of course that literacy comes later. It is also possible that reciting or writing in parallels may be good for memorizing. Another theory suggests that it is based on very ancient "finger rhymes." These are games and verses using the five fingers of one hand to make the statement in five steps, and the fingers of the other hand for elaborating or balancing it, and bringing the two hands together at the end.[27] Another suggestion is that it has a common origin in very early times with acrostic composition. Whatever its pre-literate origins, ring composition has of course been transformed with the advent of writing. For my own purposes, the question of an origin in oral literature can be left to one side. It does not need to be settled for considering the main questions about ring composition.

The arrival of literacy does not make parallelism atrophy and disappear. The prolific biblical examples of parallelism come from a very literate civilization. Albert Lord's pioneering fieldwork among illiterate Yugo-Slav peasants showed that trained bards had astonishingly long and accurate memories, though they were not interested in perfect word-for-word recall.[28] So far from requiring a mechanical memorizing of lines, even if the singer thinks he is repeating a story verbatim, the singing of it is essentially a creative interaction between the current performer and the traditional song.

Jack Goody's theory about memorizing is relevant. He associates learning by heart with early literacy; once literacy begins to be widespread it changes the whole basis for social life by redistributing power in favor of the literate. One of the effects is the establishment of schools for learning literate skills and for memorizing important texts; consequently, learning by rote is a characteristic of literate society. Evidence exists for Egyptian schools as early as the third millennium BCE. Scholars would have spent their time reading, writing, and reciting.[29]

I am more concerned to emphasize ring composition's exegetical function. It controls meaning, it restricts what is said, and in doing so it expands meanings along channels it has dug. Though it never completely escapes ambiguity, writing in a ring puts various strategies at the writer's disposal; when he chooses one path or another he ties the meaning into a recognizable, restricting context. Ring composition is not poetry but it puts syntactic-like restrictions on the writer. It is worth pausing to reflect on why restraints are necessary.

It is not just a matter of syntax, though syntax is confusing enough. In our London street a notice board tells us that "dog-fouling" is an offense. Usually, in English, when a noun qualifies a participle the noun is the object of the verb, as in wife-beating, trout-fishing, making it easy to use "wife-beater" or "trout-fisher" as the agent. Normal syntax implies that we should be looking out for some malefactor who is fouling our dogs. The trouble with words is that they do not stay the same. "It was vulgar at the beginning of the nineteenth century to mention the word 'handkerchief' on the French tragic stage. An arbitrary convention had decreed that tragic personages inhabit a world in which noses only exist to distinguish the noble Roman nose from the Greeks and Hebrews, never to be blown."[30] Words interpenetrate, as Ferdinand de Saussure liked to show. Meanings never stay the same, analogy is wild and willful, ambiguity thrives as the words tumble vertiginously through the sounds; they mix, they riddle and jump.[31]

Written words lack the support of body language, voice, and physical context. The ring convention does something to fill the interpretative gap by virtue of its symmetry, its completeness, and its patterned cross-referencing. A citation from Douglas Hofstadter brings home the problems solved by the ring form: "A word being the name of a concept, and a concept being a class of items linked by analogy, and people by nature being creative and ever finding new analogies, a word's connotations are consequently oozing continually outwards to form an ever-larger and blurrier nebula as more and more analogies are cognized as legitimate and welcomed by the culture. A table thus acquires legs, a mountain acquires a foot, ships venture into space, sopranos sing high and basses low, books have jackets, families have trees, computers have memories, salad is dressed, wine breathes, cars run, hearts dance, a storm threatens . . . ," and so on.[32]

Analogies are endless; as a pattern of analogies a ring composition constrains the multiple meanings of words. It does so by giving each stanza or section its parallel pair; the members of a pair are placed on opposite sides of the ring so that each faces the other; each indicates its pair by verbal correspondences. Thus two constructed likenesses have been selected and polished and carefully matched so as to guide the range of interpretation. You can compare the functions of ring composition to syntax: it tames wild words and firmly binds their meanings to its frame. Another function is greatly to deepen the range of reference by playing on the double meanings of words. Another of its benefits is that it is a form of play; it gives the pleasure of a game to the composer and the reader.

Some examples will show how deceptively complex a seemingly simple ring can be. I will start with a very familiar story from the book of Genesis, the Garden of Eden, which Cassuto identified as one of the little rings of which Genesis is composed.[33] The more the story is already familiar, the more the sense of surprise at the density of meaning that is packed into this form. The story seems to flow so smoothly that the strong structure of its background environment is unsuspected. It starts in an amorphous, misty, barren place that contrasts with the charming garden full of trees that God willed into being.

The story begins from before the point at which God has created man and woman (1.26–31). At first, there was no man to till the

Gn 2:5	There was no *ādām* to till the *ădāmah*.
2:7	God formed the *ādām* from the dust of the *ădāmah*,
2:15	to guard and till the garden of Eden.
2:17	The *ādām* was not to eat of the tree of knowledge.
2:21–24	To allay his loneliness God brought a partner out of the *ādām*.
	The *ādām* is now *īsh* and *ishshah*, united in perfect harmony.
2:25	They are naked (*'ărūmīm*) and free from shame.
3:1–6	But the subtle (*'ărūm*) serpent tempts them to disobey.
3:7–10	They become aware of their nakedness and feel shame.
3:16	Their harmony is spoilt: hereafter *īsh* will dominate *ishshah*.
3:19	The *ādām* must return to the *ădāmah* from which he was taken.
3:22	The *ādām* may not eat of the tree of life.
3:23	The *ādām* must till the *ădāmah* but with toil and sweat, no longer in Eden;
3:24	Eden now has a new guardian to keep the *ādām* from the tree of life.

Fig. 3. The tragedy of Adam (human being) formed from the *adamah* (soil).
Courtesy of Robert Murray.

ground. God made a man from the earth, breathed life into him, and set him in a garden with four rivers in and around it (2.4–3.24). The concept of water channeled into rivers contrasts with the initial undifferentiated swampiness. The theme seems to be very simple in English, but there is a punning play on the Hebrew word for "soil" (*adamah*) and on the Hebrew word for a human being named "Adam."

Robert Murray has selected the resonances between these two words and shown how they underpin the progress of the story (Fig. 3).[34] The panel presentation shows up the central place very clearly, verses 2.25 to 3.7–10. It is a lesson to teach us to expect subtle sophistication and to realize how much we miss in the Bible when we try to read the apparently simple stories without knowing the sounds of the Hebrew words. Note that the subject matter, the theme of return, the return of Adam to the soil, is exemplified in the ring convention itself, the end returns to the beginning. Adam was made from the soil.

Except for a slight displacement from 3.19 on, this is a clear example of a pattern that occurs in a number of places in the Bible; perfect form would be:

a

b

c

d

       e

d*

c*

b*

a*

The effect is to give special emphasis to the pivotal central point. In the Eden story, this place is occupied by the intervention of the serpent. The serpent's malice is highlighted even more by the play on two words quite different in meaning but sounding very like each other, which come in adjacent verses (2.25 and 3.1 — chapter divisions are medieval, not original, in the Hebrew Bible). These words refer respectively to the nakedness of the human pair and the slyness of the serpent. But note (very important): Hebrew has two words for "naked": one is used in contexts of sexual activity, the other, used in 2.25, always connotes vulnerability — of children and other helpless persons.

This is a superb example of a very short ring, a small ring inside a larger one. It is a blessing to have its subtleties displayed by a Hebrew scholar. I hope it whets the appetite for the macro-composition of a very large ring, such as that of Genesis or Numbers.

two

Literature is institutional; institutions establish stereotyped forms of behavior, and literature itself contributes to the selection and stereotyping process. It is useful to be able to think of genres as distinctive institutional forms within literature, among other "literary kinds."[1] They coordinate with non-literary institutional forms, set up ideals for behavior, and justify them. The readers, themselves embedded in institutional life, need to recognize the genre they are reading, so it has to make itself distinctive. Assigning a work to a genre gives the readers expectations about a literary piece, and they learn to judge whether it is a good sample.

Frank Kermode would modify the sharpness of definition that would follow from calling a genre a "literary kind": "A genre is not what used to be known as a *kind*, with rules prescribed by institutional authority; it is a context of expectation, 'an internalized probability system,'" he says, quoting a nice phrase of Leonard Meyer's.[2] A genre, Kermode goes on to say, "is the set of expectations which enables us to follow a sentence as it is spoken."[3]

There are rules. They are not imposed from outside of the literary work. They are not there first. They emerge from the first completed works. New genres are always in the making; the breach of one rule is enough to introduce a new variant. They overlap, and mix; some last a long time, some die out. It was only half a century ago that the Dutch scholar W. Otterlo produced the first systematic analysis of ring composition.[4] He noted that ring composition has passed unnoticed over the centuries until our time. His book was focused on Homeric studies, to which I have occasion to return in Chapter 8. He counts ring composition as a late archaic style that finishes around the middle of the fifth century BCE. This view is endorsed by G. B. Gray, who thought that it had been ousted by metric forms.[5] Ring composition did become obsolete. How it came to be ousted is one of the central (not wholly answered) questions of this study.

Otterlo was interested in the variety of circular structures in the *Iliad*. The *Iliad* has rings with only one "member," and rings with two or three "members." His classification of structures is chiefly concerned with the relations of the minor rings to the major ring in which they are enclosed. In the latter a main ring keeps track of the thread of the narration, picking it up again after a digression. Otterlo cites as an example the travels of Odysseus interrupted by such digressions as the hunt of Autolycus, a clearly circumscribed event, after which the poet returns to the main ring and resumes the tale of the journey.[6] Another structure is a main ring that includes minor rings containing an argument about or explanation of what is narrated. These interludes are not digressions but supplements. He goes on to identify different kinds of rings within rings.

Classification can be extended to the difference between the structure of the external enclosing ring and the structure of the rings within rings, which are predictably much shorter. I would suspect that it might be easier to make a little ring in which clusters of key words will be enough to indicate the matching parallel sections and to bring them into position. But a very elegant small ring, like that in the Garden of Eden, which I discussed in Chapter 1, cannot be easy at all. At least we can say that long pieces need more structure and more conspicuous signaling of the structure. In a short piece the word-for-word echoing is enough to match the ending to the beginning. A long composition often has to add something more to knot the ending firmly to the start. It often has an epilogue (or "latch") added after all the paralleling is done.

It is time to give examples. First, for a small ring, the heart-wrenching story of the binding of Isaac will illustrate Otterlo's interest in the ring within a ring. The story of Isaac's binding is replete with meaning, moral, theological, and emotional, and has been controversial through the ages. The literal text carries various ambiguities, especially concerning the intentions of God in commanding

Abraham to sacrifice his own son. In secular understanding both God and Abraham have very bad coverage. How can God be good if he makes such a grotesque demand? How can Abraham be good if he obeys it? Jonathan Magonet puts it as crudely as I could dare: "If we read chapter 22 alone, as unfortunately too often we do, then, if we are honest, we must conclude that God is as mad as Abraham who would obey such a God."[7]

A huge statue of Abraham, blade in hand, standing grimly over his young son, stands on the campus of Princeton University. Created by the sculptor George Segal, it is called "In Memory of May 4th, 1970, Kent State: Abraham and Isaac." Kent State is a university in Bowling Green, Ohio. When Richard Nixon announced the bombing of Cambodia in April 1970, student protests immediately followed. The National Guard was called out at Kent State, and on May 4 guards shot and killed four students.[8] That Abraham should have been cast in this brutal role in the memorial to the students' revolt testifies to the common lay interpretation (misinterpretation) of the story of Isaac. It is utterly inept: Isaac never revolted; he was to be a consenting victim, and Abraham never killed him.

The text for the binding of Isaac (Genesis 22) is summarized and arranged as a chiastic structure in Figure 4. Interpretation must focus on the question of how much Abraham understood when making preparations to obey. Many Western commentators expatiate on the anguish in the old man's heart and on the cruelty of a God who could lay such a brutal command on a loving father.[9] The characters of both Abraham and God show in a quite different light if Abraham understood what was to happen. If Abraham did know that he would never have to carry out the command, then literary, psychological, and theological speculations about his anguish are beside the point.

Jewish traditions take other lines. Abraham's total commitment to God is taken for granted. Some emphasize his unquestioning obedience. There is also a tradition that emphasizes Isaac's own consent, even his heroic desire to be the victim in the sacrifice of atonement.[10] Sebastian Brock presents a Syriac text from late antiquity that focuses

I.
God tested
Abraham & said to
him: 'Abraham!'
and he said: 'Here
I am'

2. 'Take your son, your only son, Isaac, and offer him as a burnt offering on one of the mountains of which I shall tell you. . . '		15–18. The Angel of the Lord called to Abraham a second time from heaven & said: 'Because you have done this and have not withheld your son, your only son, I will bless you indeed. . . .'
3. Preparations for going to the place of which God had told him. . . the Ass, two young men, the wood for the burnt offering and Isaac. 4. Abraham lifted up his eyes and saw the place afar off. 5. . . . told the young men to stay. . . .		14. Abraham called the name of the place 'God will provide.'
6. Took the wood for the burnt offering, laid it on Isaac, took in his hand the fire & the knife.		13. Abraham took the ram . . . offered it as a burnt offering, instead of his son.
7. So they went on both of them together: Isaac: 'Father' Abraham: 'Here I am my son' 'Behold the fire & the wood, where is the lamb for a burnt offering?' 8. 'God will see to the lamb for a burnt offering, my son.' So they went on both of them together.		13. Abraham lifted up his eyes and behind him was a ram.
9. When they came to the place of which God had told him, Abraham built the altar, laid on the wood, bound Isaac, laid him on the altar and the wood. 10. Abraham raised his hand, took the knife to slay his son.		12. 'Do not raise your hand against the lad . . . for now I know that you fear God, you have not withheld your only son.'

The Angel of the
Lord called to him
from heaven:
'Abraham,
Abraham!'
'Here I am'
II.

Fig. 4. The binding of Isaac, Genesis 22.1–18.

on Isaac's mother, Sarah.[11] As he is setting out, she knows Abraham's intention and actually gives her assent, but she does not believe for a moment he will kill his son. At parting, she tells Isaac,

> If God desires you for life, he will give orders that you live; he who is
>   the immortal Lord will not kill you.
> Now I shall boast: having offered you as a gift from my womb to him
>   who gave you to me, I shall be blessed.
> Go then, my child, be a sacrifice to God, go with your father — or
>   rather your slayer. But I have faith that your father will not become
>   your slayer, for the saviour of our souls alone is God.[12]

All the ambiguities of the story are caught by this speech.

On my reading of the ring, this is why and how Abraham earned the blessing he gained for his response to God's command, not for blind obedience but for unswerving confidence in God. Differing with respect from Kierkegaard's interpretation, it was not at all absurd to expect that God would never go back on his given word; the contrary would be absurd. God had unequivocally told Abraham that Isaac would be the progenitor of a people who would belong to him and whom he would protect. All the promises to Abraham of a numberless progeny from Sarah depended on this child's survival because it was already a miracle that at her advanced age she should have given birth at all, and clearly years had passed since then and she was not going to have any more sons. Should any disaster overtake Isaac, it would make nonsense of God's covenant with Abraham, which is at the very center of the religion.

A lesser man than Abraham on receiving this command to sacrifice the boy might suppose that God had decided to cancel plan A and was now preparing for plan B by getting rid of Isaac. But a man of such faith as Abraham's could not have forgotten the promises whose fulfillment required Isaac to survive, and he believed in a God who was true to his word.

Against the view that Abraham knew that he would not be required to sacrifice his son, some scholars would argue that nothing in the text of Genesis 22 advises the reader that Isaac was not going to be killed, and that the text does nothing to show that Abraham knew it. A close look at the ring structure quenches this criticism, however, and the ambiguity and uncertainty fade away. First, note how strongly the ring syntax puts the story in a frame of loving fathers and sons. It sets the mood for a touching scene. God refers to Abraham's beloved son; Abraham's filial relation to God is pointed by the echoing of the reply, "Here am I," twice, in verses 1, 11, when God called him; and Abraham uses the same words in verse 7, in his reply to Isaac's calling him "Father." In ring composition repetitions are markers of structure. These repeated answers have made a parallelism between two sons: Abraham becomes beloved son to God, and Isaac is Abraham's beloved son. The repeated double emphasis on paternal affection, divine and human, tells the reader to anticipate the happy outcome. It draws a clear correspondence between God as father to Abraham and Abraham as father to Isaac.

Remember also Abraham's reasons for trust. Isaac was the miracle child that his mother (too old to conceive and bear) was promised a year before his birth: "Sarah, your wife, shall bear you a son, and you shall call his name Isaac. I will establish my covenant with him as an everlasting covenant for his descendants after him" (Genesis 17.19). The covenant is the background of the story and ratifies the interpretation that fits with the established reputations of God and Abraham.

This panel form is one of the usual ways of presenting a chiastic structure. Chapter 11 is the center (ignore the asymmetry of bulk). This is the point at which the recital starts its return to the beginning. I personally do not like this presentation, partly because it is difficult to see the match between items, but mainly because the design obscures the link between beginning and ending by placing them visually as far apart as possible. I prefer to display it as a ring, so that the ending visibly joins up with the beginning, and the matching of corresponding stanzas on each side is easy to see. This would be a ring with twelve points of reference (Fig. 5).

To present this short version of the story I have picked out obvious verbal concordances and overlooked some that did not seem to mean anything in this pattern, such as Abraham twice raising his eyes.

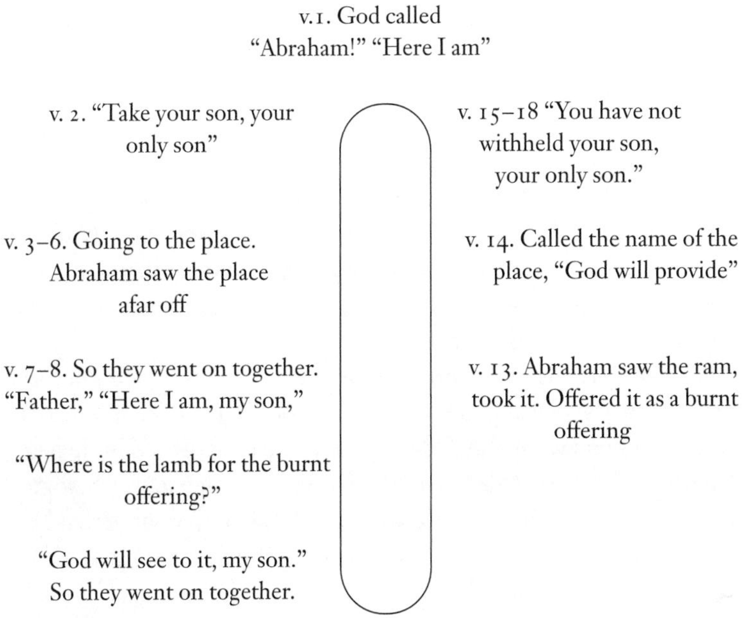

v.1. God called
"Abraham!" "Here I am"

v. 2. "Take your son, your
only son"

v. 15–18 "You have not
withheld your son,
your only son."

v. 3–6. Going to the place.
Abraham saw the place
afar off

v. 14. Called the name of the
place, "God will provide"

v. 7–8. So they went on together.
"Father," "Here I am, my son,"

v. 13. Abraham saw the ram,
took it. Offered it as a burnt
offering

"Where is the lamb for the burnt
offering?"

"God will see to it, my son."
So they went on together.

Fig. 5. The Akedah in a ring, showing the pattern of key words.

Clearly this version can be improved and elaborated. It is here to introduce the point about a ring within the ring, verses 7 and 8, which are parallel to verse 13.

Reading the binding of Isaac (Genesis 22.1–18) as a ring, we need to notice the opening phrase and its repetitions. The story opens abruptly with God calling from Heaven, "Abraham!" Then, at the most dramatic moment in verse 11, he repeats it: "Abraham!" The call is answered each time by "Here am I!" at verse 1 and verse 11, in the same words, thus making the start correspond to the midpoint. The repetition splits the ring down the middle, as in the ring diagram in Figure 5. The split into two halves is the first big clue to reading it as a ring.

At verses 15–18 we know we have come to the end because the heavenly call "Abraham!" is repeated, and also because "You have not withheld your only son" concords with verse 2. The ending has met the beginning. In between the three heavenly interventions, which open and conclude the whole and mark the middle, Abraham is preparing to obey the command. In all respects it is a standard ring form, where the ring is divided vertically by the two "Here am I" phrases. There is a clear mid-turn. No further elaboration connects the middle with the beginning and end; they are connected directly by the spoken words. This is so short a story, and it is so compact, no more needs to be said. In the big rings the mid-turn is often elaborated at length and forms another a ring in itself.

This story is one of the literary examples chosen by Erich Auerbach to illustrate the power and authority of biblical narrative, in spite of its "only rudimentary syntax."[13] He generally compares the Bible negatively with Homer's *Odyssey*, replete with syntax, rich in psychological information and sense of place and time. However, we note that both are ring structures, though he is comparing short with long rings. We can expect that for both long and short forms the ring itself provides syntax for the composition. It explains the power and authority of the biblical narration, which Auerbach extols. It also controls the interpretation.

We said that the story is split down the middle by the repeated call "Abraham!" and the answer, "Here I am!" (in verses 1 and 11). There is a first section in which the constituent verses 2 through 10 are paired with their corresponding verses in the second section, 12 to 18, on the other side of the mid-turn. Notice how the author has placed a little ring within the bigger ring. The words "So they went on, both of them together" are repeated to make an envelope, or *inclusio*:

A   So they went on both of them together. [v. 6]
B   Isaac: "My Father,"
C   Abraham: "Here am I, my son." [v. 7]
B′   "Behold, the fire and the wood. Where is the lamb for a burnt offering?"
C′   "God will see to the lamb for a burnt offering, my son." [v. 8]
A′   So they went on, both of them together.

The four lines inside the bracketing words of A and A' are the dialogue between father and son, two sentences for each speaker.[14] At the C and C' lines Abraham repeats the words "my son" and affirms his confidence in God. Father and son walking along, "both of them together," conveys intimacy and affectionate trust but also much more. By repeating the words "Here am I" but adding "my son," the loving relation between Abraham and Isaac makes a parallel with the relation of Abraham and God: it indicates that Abraham is like a beloved son to God. This spreads the trusting intimacy of the repeated phrase "They went on, both of them together." The affectionate wording of the internal ring sets the mood of the piece. I maintain that it tells us that Abraham knows what it is all about and that he has nothing to fear for his son.

Isaac knows he is unique and beloved, and he almost certainly has known from infancy that God's plan for a covenanted people depends entirely on his own survival. The double ring tells us eventually that there is no reason to suppose they are speaking to each other in anguish. It is like a family performance. Father and son support each other in demonstrating their perfect confidence in God's love and goodness. Abraham knows full well that God has set all his plans for a people to worship him on this one boy's progeny. Isaac is destined to grow up and found a lineage.

The clinching point is that the positioning of the internal ring is a pointer: it is placed exactly opposite the position of the ram caught by his horns (see Fig. 4). Outside of the literary frame Isaac's question "Where is the lamb?" might seem to be devastating. But when Abraham, unperturbed, gives his cool answer, "God will provide it," and the parallel points across the diagram to Abraham's finding the ram trapped in the thicket, his answer is validated. As the bard sings verses 13 and 14 the listeners will catch the words "for a burnt offering" repeated, and will thrill with recognition.

The double-ring form has set a mood that is not anguished or suspenseful; Abraham is not in agony, God is not unkind, the child is not afraid (Fig. 6). God is content that Abraham has demonstrated

Fig. 6. Father and son confident together. Drawn by Pat Novy.

that he knew what would happen; he trusted in God's keeping his word, and he was right to do so, and so was Sarah.

There are also cross-references and smaller chiastic twists inside the big ring. For example, verses 11 through 16 start and end with God's call, so enclosing the whole of the second section as a second ring, or a subset of the first. Verses 7 and 13, and 4 and 13 are also elegantly cross-linked, creating a tightly integrated whole. I hope that these short examples show how richly worked the small rings can be. Placing them here will help me in the next chapter to describe how a ring composition, large or small, is constructed.

After Otterlo and Vladimir Propp, no one should be surprised to find sophistication and subtlety in early literature, as well as observance of elaborate rhetorical conventions.[15] The strongly knit composition explains why the ring does not easily yield its meaning at the first reading and perhaps explains why it has fallen out of use. (More of this in Chapter 10.)

A literary form is a resource; it can be used to declare whatever the writers want to publish abroad. It comes into fashion and goes out. The society itself, not the instruments of expression it has produced, puts constraints on the thought of its members, if only by the sheer need to live together in peace. The ring is obviously a demanding construction. The initial question for this study is why people whose life is relatively simple would want to write in such a complex way. Part of the answer is that however simple the form of community, the members normally need to distinguish a high style from the low-style speech that serves for work or domestic life. Ring composition is used for ceremonial speeches, victory odes, funeral orations, and joyful celebrations. It is also the common form for solemnly reciting myths of origin, or for entertainment by wandering bards. It is very old, and it is extant still in different parts of the world.

Complex conventions of writing or speaking fulfill a role in validating a message. Religious doctrine tends always to be under challenge. Skeptics or rivals will be alert to contest it. No wonder that religious themes should inspire very elegant writing and, in their high periods, unsurpassed literary and artistic technique. A well-crafted composition is its own authentication. The elaboration is not just for fun; it is the way to say that something is important, something serious needs to be said, there is a message that must be heard. It must be unambiguous, so it is surrounded on all sides with compatible materials and packed deep into a big container.

We need to recall how any community may be aware of its own fragility. So much work has to go into its maintenance, and dissensions arise so easily. Angry departures threaten to split the group, and quiet defections happen all the time. Even at the basic level of keeping up its numbers, a community is vulnerable to strife. Disagreement about facts tears it apart. But facts by themselves will not force a decisive verdict. Interpretation is open in principle, but the members who want the community to stay together, and at peace, will try to achieve agreement.

Those ancient peoples whose writings puzzle us have struggled hard against intellectual confusion by establishing their own foundations of knowledge. Strong taboos helped to maintain their cosmology. The mere fact that their civilization has persisted shows that they have held disruptive intellectual challenge in check. Blank areas of knowledge protected by rules of silence uphold the coherence of their intercourse. To preserve their old certainties they would have had to control the young and keep foreigners out. The better they are insulated from the outside, the easier it is for an isolated community to hold to their common knowledge of the world's regularities. Spared challenge from beyond their walls, they can lay their cosmologies on logical foundations and entrench them by regular practice. Their taboos and purity rules would hold the foundations steady.

But these solutions to social problems imply that a stranger's claims to hospitality are inevitably subject to scrutiny. He needs to give evidence of his claimed identity. To do so, he may have to recite a long kinship genealogy, in which the least mistake will damage his claims. If he is to pass as a sage, he may be required to name the sages under whom he has studied. Display of literary skills is an additional kind of validation.[16] For the traveler needing friends abroad, a show of literary authority may be as good as a letter of introduction. I suggest that this may be one context for explaining why ring composition would be highly elaborate and difficult to master.

Competence in literary skills would be one of the proofs of worth. Simply by virtue of its symmetry and intricate completeness, the ring form conveys authority and prestige. This would be one of the advantages of a dominant literary form in societies with simple technology and weak coordination. Durkheim's argument was that these are precisely the kinds of communities that need to have shared meanings to give a basis to their otherwise fragile solidarity.[17] Such communities absolutely need to settle on some agreed meanings.

Competition for a following is one of the ways this is done. A large following gives prestige and authority to the winners.[18] The very complexity of the conventions of ring composition suggests competition among the poets, teachers, and songwriters. Competition for prestige is one of the drives that hold society together. For an example of competition in poetic competence, consider the Somali, people of a warrior nation who compose and passionately love poetry. They greatly admire an accomplished poet; they deride an unskilled one. Their judgments are based on elaborate poetic forms deploying formidably complex rules of alliteration. "In every hemistich of a poem at least one word has to begin with a chosen consonant or with a vowel . . . only identical initial consonants are regarded as alliterative . . . with one another and no substitution by similar words is admissible. All initial vowels count as alliterative with each other, and again, this principle is most strictly observed. The same alliteration is maintained throughout the poem . . . if the alliterative sound of the poem is the consonant g, in every hemistich there is one word beginning with g."[19]

A man aspiring to leadership among the Somali can win support only if he can demonstrate his mastery of these fiendishly difficult literary exercises. This is a nation where politicians must compete as poets. By their poetry they earn esteem and attract followers. Their political hustings are great poetry sessions where poets recite to highly critical audiences.

Language is not self-authenticating. As we listen we consider whether to believe the words we hear, whether we have understood them right, whether to act on them. What is true is not always said convincingly. In the summer of 2003, as I was writing this, the British government was acutely embarrassed by the charge of having spoken deceiving words about the need to go to war. Scrutinizing the words does not help; they can bear two meanings: as a warning of danger, desperately urgent, or as merely cautionary. Written words are not supported by body language, voice, and physical context. They lack that foundation. This is where poetry can help: a show of literary authority may be as good as a show of independence or valor.

This would be one of the advantages of a high-style literary form in societies with simple technology and weak coordination. All communities need to have shared meanings. A set of literary conventions (the more complex the better) is necessary for the itinerant teacher or holy man.

three

If ring composition is really rooted in our universal mental heritage, why do we have to have all this explained? Why do we ourselves not compose ring structures all the time? and everywhere? Parallelism has had a universal distribution over the globe, so why does it feebly give way to other compositional forms? Why do the old-fashioned rings no longer make sense? More directly to my theme, why do ring compositions get so badly treated by Western scholars? And going back a step further, why are ring compositions so difficult for us to read?

Moving now to show how a ring is composed will help to lay the basis for answering this question. I have put off this chapter too long. We will now consider some of the technical problems in composing in rings. When the sequence of a composition seems to be jumbled, the question is, "What is this piece doing here?" One satisfying answer to this is: "It is here to complete the pattern of the book." Or, "Its position just here cues the reader to see a correspondence across the book." Or else: "The positioning of this piece enriches the meaning by pointing to analogies."

It is time to be more precise about what makes a text into a ring. Definition is frustrated by the great variety of ring structures; some are quite loose and free, some are very strict. We know already that a ring composition is known by the ending coming back to match the beginning. From this feature the name "ring" derives, but there are other features of ring composition that follow from it.

Chiasmus is a structuring device that inverts the ordering of words. A major ring is a triumph of chiastic ordering. "The phenomenon of inverted word orders," as Welch and McKinlay's impressive *Chiasmus Bibliography* demonstrates, is one of the prime indicators of the ring.[1] The other prime test of a well-turned ring is the loading of meaning on the center and the connections made between the center and the beginning; in other words, the center of a polished ring integrates the whole. Welch's concluding chapter lists fifteen criteria that can be used to measure the strength or weakness of the chiastic structure in a given text. The most interesting of these (and the most debatable) is his effort to distinguish a chiastic ordering that just happened, without any authorial intent, from one that has been deliberately planned. He warns against the "intentional fallacy," the idea that any discernible pattern in the text must have been devised intentionally.[2]

To this I demur, finding it hard to believe that a large poem could be chiastically ordered without anyone having knowingly created the structure. To my mind it is deliberate, which invites us to ask, what this form of literature is meant to achieve when it is used for long literary exercises? Are the restrictions onerous? Why are they accepted and the rules obeyed?

I can think of very short chiastic forms arising spontaneously in compositions or in snatches of conversation. In my childhood we knew a countryman who used to speak chiastically. Waiting for him to work through an idea was slow. In the following speech the first and last lines correspond; the order of words is inverted. Like a true ring the message is cupped in the center, C, and framed by parallels, AA′, and BB′, and the first and last lines are virtually the same.

> A These young plants don't want too much water;
>> B Don't water them every day,
>>> C Water them every other day. [Here is the kernel of the message.]
>> B′ If you water them on Monday, do nowt on Tuesday, water them on Wednesday.
> A′ Too much water isn't good for these young plants.

This was quite spontaneous. Welch mentions the story of a queen who answered twelve questions, starting with the twelfth and working her way back to the first. It seems a natural way to remember a list. Even longer chiastic passages are probably not too difficult to produce off the cuff. They are found in the Bible, plentifully scattered through most of the books of the Pentateuch and histories and also through the New Testament. Roland Meynet usefully confirms that this style makes reading of the Bible difficult for the modern reader.[3] They have been much discussed, following in the path of Lund's classic *Chiasmus in the New Testament*, which gives a survey of earlier work.[4] But most of these examples are content to pick out little parallelisms and forbear to test the structure of a whole book.

Attempts to identify the macro-compositional form that controls a long poem or a whole book by giving it an all-embracing frame are fewer. It is a massive undertaking in which Cassuto led the way with looking for ring forms in the beginning of Genesis.[5] I note also Jonathan Magonet's analysis of the book of Jonah as a system of parallelisms.[6] An outstanding exception is Gary Rendsburg in *The Redaction of Genesis*. He reveals an all-inclusive chiastic macro-structure that incorporates the whole book of Genesis. He displays the ring structure while systematically checking on the observance of the conventions for ring composition that I am about to list.[7]

This analysis has been frequently applied to the New Testament. Some of the analyses are a bit thin and scrappy. There are outstanding exceptions. One of the finest is John Bligh's commentary on Paul's letter to the Galatians. Bligh is convinced that the whole composition is arranged in chiastic form, and he demonstrates the case with meticulous scholarship.[8]

The author of a major ring needs to know how to expand the structure of a few bare lines into the structure of a long poem or of a book. Following Welch's general invitation to go further with the work he has begun, and following his example of a list of fifteen criteria, I have found that the following seven indicators are enough to show how ring composers identify and signal the literary kind they are embarked upon. The minimum seven rules are just too many to be of the spontaneous, unintended kind of inverted sequence.

To summarize, the first indication of a ring composition is that the end corresponds to the beginning. The link between start and finish signals completion. If there is no such tie-up, the composition is not in a ring. The correspondences are indicated by key words, as we saw in the story of Isaac. The key words or word clusters indicate thematic parallels that appear in both items of a pair. Part of the strategy of construction is to divide the whole piece into two parallel halves that will be chiastically related. The pattern is ABC for the first sequence and CBA for the second. Reversing the order is the technique for bringing the ending back to the beginning. The second part can be said to have turned around, or crossed over. The mid-turn is written so that it makes correspondences with the prologue and with the ending. When the whole poem or book is gathered together in the middle, and referred to again at the end, the result is a well-integrated composition.

The formal closure that makes it a ring would be an easy requirement, if that were all. The turning and closure by return to the start is the commonest rule for almost any composition — a beginning, middle, and an end. But, as I have just said, closure is not the only, or even the principal, condition for a ring. Essentially, ring composition is a double sequence of analogies. First a sequence is laid down, then at a certain point the sequence stops and the series turns around and a new sequence works its way backward, step by step toward the beginning. This puts each member of the new series parallel to its opposite number in the first series, so the return journey reverses the order of the outgoing journey. The longer ring forms tend to embellish the mid-turn with an elaborate commentary. A well-marked turning point is a sign of a well-designed ring composition (Fig. 7). Sometimes it takes the form of a minor ring. Sometimes it is so long as to mislead the reader about its place in a larger structure.

It is not difficult to recognize a mid-turn if you are alert to the functions it performs for the piece as a whole. As in any well-developed literary form, the conventions answer to specific technical problems. Other bards or rival writers will judge the work by its skill in resolving these problems. They will expect symmetry and balance, and they will judge how well the ending slots on to the start. To bring the pre-ordained ending elegantly back to the beginning is not so easy as it may sound. One of the special literary merits of a ring is to anticipate its own form of closure from the beginning.

The Meaning is in the Middle.

Fig. 7. The scroll. Drawn by Pat Novy.

I have abstracted the following seven rules or conventions from long ring compositions. They are not rules in the sense of there being something hard and fast about them. Breach carries no penalties, but insofar as they are commonly observed they are like rules. They are responses to the technical problems of coming back gracefully to the start. Other technical problems arise out of the solution adopted for circumventing the first.

1. *Exposition or prologue:* There is generally an introductory section that states the theme and introduces the main characters. You can call it a prologue. It sets the stage, sometimes the time and the place. Usually its tone is bland and somewhat enigmatic. It tells of a dilemma that has to be faced, a command to be obeyed, or a doubt to be allayed. Above all, it is laid out so as to anticipate the mid-turn and the ending that will eventually respond to it.

2. *Split into two halves:* If the end is going to join the beginning the composition will at some point need to make a turn toward the start. The convention draws an imaginary line between the middle and the beginning, which divides the work into two halves, the first, outgoing, the second, returning. In a long text it is important to accentuate the turn lest the hasty reader miss it, in which case the rest of the carefully balanced correspondences will also be missed.

3. *Parallel sections:* After the mid-turn the next challenge for the composer of a ring is to arrange the two sides in parallel. This is done by making separate sections that are placed in parallel across the central dividing line. Each section on one side has to be matched by its corresponding pair on the other side. In practice the matching of sections often contains surprises; items are put into concordance that had not previously been seen to be similar. Parallelism gives the artist opportunities of taking the text to deeper levels of analogy. When the reader finds two pages set in parallel that seem quite disparate, the challenge is to ask what they may have in common, not to surmise that the editor got muddled.

4. *Indicators to mark individual sections:* Some method for marking the consecutive units of structure is technically necessary. The primary problem is to make clear to the reader or listener where one section stops and the next begins. Otherwise the pattern fades out. There are various methods. Key words always carry a lot of the weight of marking the sections. In a long composition the author will also have resort to specific signals to indicate beginnings or endings of the sections. Only when these have been found can the meanings that have been packed together be sorted out. One method is to close off each section by repeating a refrain, like the chorus line of a folk song.

Another method is to use alternation to mark the beginnings and endings of sections. The book of Numbers solves the problem of marking individual sections by using a very strong principle of alternation. The whole book is organized as a system of strictly alternating narratives and laws. It thus boldly solves the technical problem: the general question of how to recognize where a section starts and where it ends becomes the question of how to recognize a narrative, and where it starts and stops, and how to recognize a legal section. In the *Iliad* Homer organizes the Trojan War by alternating nights and days. The strong patterning works to guide the interpretation.

5. *Central loading:* The turning point of the ring is equivalent to the middle term, C, that is the middle term of a chiasmus, AB / C / BA. Consequently, much of the rest of the structure depends on a well-marked turning point that should be unmistakable. One clue that the middle has been reached is that it uses some of the same key word clusters that were found in the exposition. As the ending also accords with the exposition, the mid-turn tends to be in concordance with them both. Then the whole piece is densely interconnected.

6: *Rings within rings:* As Otterlo pointed out, the major ring may be internally structured by little rings. Some rings emphasize the division into two halves by making each half a ring (as demonstrated in Genesis 22, the binding of Isaac). A large book often contains many small rings. They may come from different sources, times, and authors. One large ring can be composed entirely from minor rings strung together in groups. This practice makes the ring form ideal for incorporating old materials, as in the Bible. For examples of rings inside a ring, refer to the stories of the shield of Achilles in the *Iliad*, Balaam in the book of Numbers, and Isaac's binding in Genesis.

7: *Closure at two levels:* By joining up with the beginning, the ending unequivocally signals completion. It is recognizably a fulfillment of the initial promise. Just arriving at the beginning by the process of inverted ordering is not enough to produce a firm closure. The final section signals its arrival at the end by using some conspicuous key words from the exposition. Verbal repetitions indicate that the first and the last section match in other ways. Most importantly, there also has to be thematic correspondence: the original mission turns out to have been successful, or it has failed; the setting forth is matched by the journey ended; the command to go into battle at the start is completed by news of the battle being finally won, or lost. The exposition will have been designed to correspond to the ending. When it comes the reader can recognize it as the ending that was anticipated in the exposition. In my opinion this sort of double literary closure is not going to happen accidentally.

The seven conventions are drawn from the style of large ring form prevalent in the literature of the Mediterranean eastern hinterland in the eighth to the fourth centuries. These have been for me the most accessible. But this is not the only form of ring; many different regional styles have developed over time. For example, the pattern of the Indian Sufi romance *Madhumālatī* (by Manjhan, A.D. 1545) belongs to a different set of conventions (Fig. 8). *Madhumālatī* is a mystical romance built on four triangles. It is certainly a long and a complex ring. It demonstrates how a system of parallels can hold the composition together by adding great depth and range to the meaning of the words as their mutual echoing draws distant contexts together.

To return to the seven conventions, when a piece conforms to them it is easy to recognize the central place and the parallel arrangement of the sections on either side. Then the interpretation is safe. It should be difficult to misinterpret the fully integrated ring or to disagree on what it is about; the parallels hold the meanings in place. The method is good for laying emphasis. As a kind of syntax, the ring form brings ambiguity under control and reduces confusion. And knowledge of the construction usually changes prior interpretations.

However, famous epics or speeches in ring form seem to have had a tendency to grow; minor rings are so easy to incorporate. The tale within the tale can be elaborated so as to sharpen the point of the whole composition, bringing an added elegance and enrichment. But too many minor rings may distract the reader's attention from the main movement along the major (inclusive) ring. The clarity of what Leonard Muellner calls the metonymic or the "syntagmatic axis" may be clouded.[9] In the Homeric examples that he considers, the relation

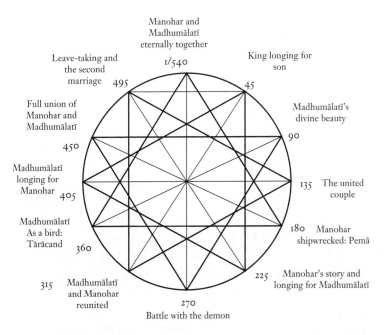

Fig. 8. The Four Triangles. From Aditya Behl and Simon Weightman,
trans., *Madhumālatī: An Indian Sufi Romance*
(Oxford: Oxford University Press, 2001). By permission of Oxford
University Press.

of one episode to the next is like that of one stanza to the rest in
nursery rhymes, the last episode incorporating the whole sequence, as
in "The House That Jack Built." I am not sure that this is always the
case. But it is true that the outer shell of the major ring, the frame
made by the largest *inclusio*, has a strong incorporative effect.

By following the formal ring structure the narrator can take the
opportunity of a differentiated shaping of the theme. There is scope
for mood change. The mood may change in keeping with the twofold
structure of the ring. The first series may develop a problem, show a
tragedy, or present a puzzle, the central place may be the site of a
major crisis, then the second series may deepen the mood or lighten it
until the final denouement is reached.

Such a structure is very clear in the book of Numbers. In the story in section V the people of Israel are in the desert, complaining about God and Moses. They dare to compare their present hardships with the good food they enjoyed in Egypt (11.1). God in anger answers them with a great fire. Nonetheless, they complain a second time, "O that we had meat to eat! We remember the fish we ate in Egypt for nothing, the cucumbers, the melons, the leeks, the onions and the garlic" (11.5), and also complain about the manna (11.6–9). Their complaints made God angry again (11.10), but he brought them quails (11.31–32), and then as they ate so lustfully he was angry and smote them with plague (11.33). This all takes place in chapter 11 on the first side of the mid-turn. On the other side of the mid-turn, in chapter 20.2–5, which is placed in parallel to 11, the people complain again, this time for water. This time the mood is kinder; God is not angry; he makes Moses strike water for them out of the rock (20.7–11).

When it is engaged in reading a structure of parallels the brain is doing its everyday exercise. Can the same be said of the return of the ending to the beginning? The words we use in everyday speech for describing the process are suggestive. When the ring has gone from the middle to the beginning it has achieved a formal completion. The task of composing the ring has been finished. As I have said, it is usually accompanied by semantic completion, such as tying up the loose themes of a narrative. The ending section has to refer explicitly to what was announced in the opening passages and to what has come to pass in the course of the poem. It brings matters to a close by distributing their just deserts to the characters or by reconciling them by fulfilling curses or promises, making prophecies come true, pointing out that the original mission has been accomplished or harmony restored. This is indirect support for Jakobson's argument that parallelism (and the chiastic structure) is hardwired in the brain.

Does the closing of the ring imply a closure of the narrative events? If so, is the closure final? The series of rings may carry the sense of being caught in successive rings without end. All the prospects may be fixed at the end, as they were foretold at the beginning. In some cultures it may be usual for the story to have shown transformations along the way, so that after the end more transformations may be expected.

For example, the prologue of the book of Numbers shows the people of Israel preparing to set out for the Promised Land. As we will see in the next chapters, it anticipates fighting and promises land at the end. By the end of Numbers many subplots have opened, developed, and ended. At the very end, the people of Israel have reached the Jordan and partitioned the land among themselves, tribe by tribe. At this point Moses reports that God has said (three times): "each of the tribes of the people of Israel shall cleave to its own inheritance" (36.7–10). This ending is an opening on the new life, which is to be described in Joshua and Chronicles. Likewise, the ending of the *Iliad* is conciliatory, as we shall see in due course.

The ring structure itself may suggest a cosmology of eternal return, or it could suggest ending and renewal. We can but look to observe whether the concluding mood is hopeful or grim. The point is that the rhetorical form does not impose any particular mood for the ending. The general impression is that the ring is a literary form that is good for reflecting on, and for establishing a long view.

When we come to chapter 7 of the *Iliad* we must be struck by how closely Homer's poem conforms to these rules of composition. This confirms that these rules are not a form of regulation that would block the creative freedom of the performing poet. Gregory Nagy insists on the element of spontaneity. He comments on bardic performance, saying: "Song is inherently recurrent and recomposed, much as every new spring is a joyous event of inherent recurrence and recomposition."[10] There is no contradiction so long as we know that the prescriptions of poetic form are a stimulus, not a constraint. As Alastair Fowler says of the rules of genre, "The very mention of prescriptive genres will have raised specters of inhibited creativity. . . . Great writers have found a challenge in genre rules, while minor or invertebrate talents have been positively supported by them, as by armatures."[11]

Douglas Hofstadter's big book on problems of translation, *Le Ton Beau de Marot*, offers a discussion of the relation of poetic form to poetic metaphor.[12] He trounces the idea that the essence of a poem is the sequence of metaphors; the form is essential. He lambasts Vladimir Nabakov for trying to translate Pushkin without representing the original structure of the poetry. However difficult it may be to capture the Russian poetic form in English, Hofstadter insists that nothing less will do justice to the task. And moreover, the constraints of rhyme and scansion do not restrict but rather spur the creative impulse. He quotes approvingly another translator of Pushkin, James Falen, on the topic of formal structure: "a translator positions himself, in a sense, on the work's home ground and imposes upon himself a useful discipline for the journey. Furthermore, he is thereby constrained, as was the poet himself, to seek solutions without self-indulgence, to find variety within oneness, and to earn a freedom within the bondage of the form. The very rigidity of the stanzaic structure can bring at times a fruitful tension to the words with which the form is made manifest, and the economy of expression it enforces upon the translator will sometimes reward him with an unexpected gift."[13]

Greatly to my purpose is Falen's tiny poem that Hofstadter received in a letter, called an "odelet" to constraints:

Every task involves constraint,
Solve the thing without complaint;
There are magic links and chains
Forged to loose our rigid brains.
Structures, strictures, though they bind,
Strangely liberate the mind.[14]

We should add the sense of liberation, or of intellectual excitement and play, to the list of good reasons that the antique poets had for following the conventions of ring composition.

The book of Numbers has the reputation of a disorderly, unstructured book. If the reader thinks that all the books of the Pentateuch enjoy equal esteem, it will be a surprise to learn that the great nineteenth-century commentator Julius Wellhausen regarded the book of Numbers as a kind of attic used for storing biblical materials that did not fit into the other books. It was a junk room for the rest of the Pentateuch. As an anthropologist, my own reading is the exact contrary. This book turns out to be another example of what Glenn Most has described as the "Pindar problem" for Western Greek classicists: the misinterpretation of the text due to a misunderstanding of its structure.[1] Numbers' problem is the same: a poet highly esteemed in his period is found to be quite impenetrable in modern times. I maintain that Numbers is not a muddle; it is a highly structured ring composition (Box 1). The book only seems disorderly because moderns are not used to reading in rings.

According to the list of conventions given in the previous chapter, a ring composition needs to have an exposition, a split into two halves, a central place or mid-turn matched to the exposition, identifiable parallel series, and an ending. After the ending there may be added a "latch." The piece may also contain smaller rings. Because it takes work to make a ring we can assume that the author intends the listener or reader to appreciate the structure. To do that, we first need to identify its building blocks. If the reader or audience is unable to distinguish one section from the next the whole thing falls into a muddle.

Numbers uses the principle of alternation very simply. A section on laws is followed by a section of narratives, then laws, then narratives all the way round. (My book *In the Wilderness* expounds the arrangement of Numbers so I hope there is no need to go into detail here.)[2]

Box 1. Numbers conforms to the seven conventions of ring composition.

Convention 1. The Exposition (or Prologue)

Chapters 1 to 4 clearly qualify as an exposition. They lay out the three main themes that will be developed through the rest of the book and will turn up again at the end. The opening theme is the order of the twelve tribes descended from the twelve sons of Jacob. The Lord tells Moses to number the tribes of Israel so that they can set out in marching formation on the journey to the banks of the Jordan. As this book follows on Exodus in the canonical order, it is obvious that they are summoned to fight their way from Sinai to the Promised Land, where they will find their inheritance (Exodus 3.8,17).

The exposition defines the status of the Levites. They will have to be counted separately. They are relegated to the role of temple servants. In this dignified but subservient destiny God has ordained that they must always be under the command of the priests, Aaron and his sons (Numbers 3.9, 10).

The third and most important theme is the sanctity of the tabernacle and the need to protect it from all profane contact. The people are warned that anyone who encroaches on the tabernacle will die. The narrative will stick faithfully to the elaboration of these initial themes.

This exposition has a grim tone; danger is in the air, danger from God's anger at encroachment on the tabernacle. The Lord tells Moses not to let the Levite family of Kohathites be destroyed (4.17), a point that will culminate in high drama in the middle section when Korah, a member of that tribe, is killed dramatically (but his brethren survive). I will say no more about this point here because the match in Numbers between exposition and mid-turn will be the main theme of the next chapter.

Convention 2. Split into Two Halves

In Numbers the mid-turn is at chapters 16 and 17 (ring section 7 in Fig. 9). After that point the text starts to work back to the beginning. This is the device that enables the sections of the first half to relate to their matching pair in the second half.

Convention 3. Identifiable Sections

We have noted that in a short poem the attentive audience can begin after the midpoint to hear repeated clusters of words that had been heard in the first half. The repetitions are clues to finding matched verses that indicate the ABCBA form. Simple verbal clues by themselves, however, are not reliable for finding the structure of a long book. Numbers makes a special point of ending each section with strongly chiastic verses.

Convention 4. Indicators

In addition to verbal clues a long book like Numbers also needs to use other, more discriminating devices to make units of structure abundantly clear. Numbers is built on the principle of alternating sections; law and narrative alternate throughout in clearly identifiable ways.

Convention 5. Central Place

Numbers makes a big climactic moment at its central place, chapters 16 and 7. This is where the Levites stage their revolt against Moses and Aaron, the joint authority under which they have been ceremonially placed in the exposition. This is where Moses' authority is justified by God. When Moses asks for a sign of divine support, the ringleaders are swallowed up by an earthquake. And this is where the authority of Aaron is asserted by the miracle of the flowering rod. In the book of Numbers the rule of loading the meaning onto the central place is fully observed. Here it gives a very political meaning to the whole book that is not the usually accepted one. There is understandable confusion insofar as the central place does not refer to the ending, nor conversely does the ending make reference to the Levites' rebellion, which fills the central place.

Convention 6. Rings within Rings

In the middle of the journey of the Israelites to the east, the story is interrupted by the story of Balaam, the foreign prophet through whose mouth God delivers prophecies of a glorious destiny for Israel.

Convention 7. Closure, the Ending

In general terms Numbers has achieved full thematic closure. By the end, three leaders have died, the people of Israel have followed the pillar of fire and cloud, they have fought off the Canaanites and arrived at the banks of the Jordan, the mission has been accomplished. Moses has fulfilled his life task; his eyes have seen the Promised Land that they are about to enter. At the very end of the book, in chapter 35, the people of Israel are reckoning the borders and distributing the land to eleven of the twelve tribes as if nothing had happened since the original numbering.

The Levites, who have figured so prominently in the exposition (as subordinates) and in the mid-turn (as rebels), are not forgotten in the ending. In chapter 35 God tells Moses to allot them cities and pastures, very necessary since they have no claim to tribal territory. The conclusion thus makes the necessary link with the exposition, but it omits the mid-turn. I discuss this further in Chapter 5.

Though there are thirteen sections in all, at this stage I need to present only the first twelve. The last one is the latch, which ought to clip the two sequences firmly together.

At an early stage of my research on Numbers, after I had identified the alternating sections I did not know how they should be arranged in relation to each other. I wondered what the number 12 represented in the editor's thought. Perhaps it referred to the lunar calendar, a twelve-month year, with an optional intercalary month when the days needed to be realigned. The latter, I thought, might be represented by the latch of the book. I looked at zodiacal circles, but I saw no light. Then I received a letter from David Meijers, who explained that the months of the year were associated with twelve principles of the universe, the *sephirot*, arranged in a circle, with two new years facing each other, one in the first month and the other in the seventh.[3] As soon as I organized the distinctive sections of Numbers in this fashion the pattern was justified by the concordances that shone out of the text.

Looking at the diagram in Figure 9 and reading the sections consecutively down the columns, we notice that the mid-turn is at 7, an odd number. This means that the sequence in the second column starts with an even number, 8, which pairs with 6 on the other side. Each of the even numbers pairs with an even number, and likewise each odd one with an odd. I take that as a signal to read them synoptically. When we find that the even-numbered sections report the laws given by God to Moses, and that the odd numbers are all narratives about the desert journey, the cue to read them across is unmistakable. They are a set of five parallel pairs, and we find that they are parallel in more senses than the simple pairing of odd and even numbering. Numbers has packed the themes of the book into five parallel rungs (Fig. 9).

Any serious reader will want to know the evidence for my claim that the sections have been laid down in parallel. Not only I myself but also David Goodman have to answer how we came to these firm conclusions. He arrived at an early point to help me with the Hebrew text on precisely this question. Table 2, showing numbered sections arranged in their parallels, provides the main part of the evidence.

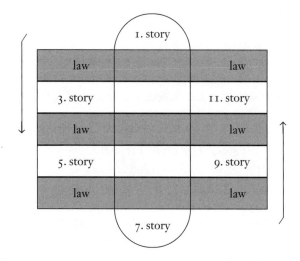

Fig. 9. Stories and laws alternating through the ring.

David Goodman found that the Hebrew text marks the separate sections in the book with syntactic, verbal, and structural signals.[4] The narrative sections have a distinctive beginning. Each opens with a time, a place, and a person or a community involved in the story. The "when, where, and who" rule is not hard and fast throughout. Sections VII and XI start by saying "who" but not "where" or "when" the event took place; section IX says "who" and "where" but not "when." Moreover, the time-space-community indicators are not exclusively used for marking the shift of style; they sometimes appear in the middle of certain main narrative sections, marking internal divisions.[5] This makes it harder for the would-be ring master. But the legal sections (the even numbers) provide backup as they have their own distinctive beginning just where a narrative section ends. Box 2 lists and quotes the "when," "where," and "who" statements that open the narrative sections.

The usual formula for beginning a legal section is: "The Lord said to Moses, Command [or 'Tell,' or 'Say to'] the people of Israel . . ." This is used in all the legal rungs beginning at chapters 5.1, 10.1, 15.1,

28.1, and 33.50. The only exception is chapter 18, which varies with "The Lord said to Aaron." The variation may have good reason since it follows the great vindication of Aaron's authority in chapter 17.

The trick is not to look for matched themes until the formal pairing has been found. The concordances arrived at by these means are impressive. For example, there is a purely formal correspondence between the first two matched sections, the command to expel lepers in section II, the first case, and to expel the Canaanites in the pairing section, XII. An example for this exercise is the relation between section II (chapters 5 and 6) and section XII (chapters 33–35). Chapter 5 gives laws about sins that break faith with the Lord. The sinner must confess and make restitution. If there is no one to whom restitution can be made, he pays it to the priest (5.5–10). Then follow two cases. The first is that of a woman accused of adultery: she may have sinned, but there is no witness; she was not caught in the act, but her husband suspects her. The jealous husband must bring his wife to the priest with a small cereal offering. The priest recites a conditional curse. She will go unharmed if she is innocent, but if she is guilty her reproductive organs will be damaged. She must say "Amen" to the curse, he writes it out, washes off his writing into a bowl of water and makes her drink it. The curse, accepted and internalized by the accused, has placed the question of guilt in God's hands. Now her husband can watch her body — if it rots he will know his suspicions were well founded. If she survives, she is proved innocent and can go on with her life.

In the same section chapter 6 seems to make another complete break with the context. It deals with the law for the Nazirite, a man or woman who has taken a vow to be separate to the Lord. Nazirites must not touch the juice of grape or take any strong drink, must never shave the head, and must never go near a dead body. These are the conditions of their special sacred status, which they will lose if they break any of the laws. What is a Nazirite to do if someone suddenly touches him as he falls down dead just beside him? The rest of the chapter details the sacrifices he must perform to annul the defilement that he has unwittingly incurred.

Table 2. Numbers' pattern of parallels, sections II–XII.
Key words have been underlined.

Laws: II: 5.2–3, <u>Put lepers out of the camp,</u> that they may not defile the camp <u>in the midst of which I dwell.</u> Rite for wife accused of adultery by her husband. 6, Nazirite's <u>unintended</u> corpse contact. 6.22, Peroration, Aaron's blessing: "and so they will put my name on the People of Israel and I will bless them."	Laws: XII: 35.34, Peroration, "<u>for I the Lord dwell in the</u> midst of the people of Israel." 34, Distribute the land by lot. 35, Forty-eight cities for Levites, six cities of refuge; law of <u>unintended</u> manslaughter. 33.50, <u>Drive out the Canaanites.</u>
Narrative: III: 7, <u>Offering of the princes of Israel to the Tabernacle,</u> tribe by tribe. 8, Light lamps, consecrate Levites. 9, Passover, the guiding cloud. <u>Setting out on the journey from Sinai.</u>	Narrative: XI: 31–33, victory against Midianites, purify warriors, captives, captured treasure, and animals. <u>The Captains' Offering of gold to the Tabernacle.</u> 32, Reuben and Gad settle in Gilead. 33, <u>Summary of journeys from Egypt to the banks of Jordan.</u>
Laws: IV: 10.1–11, <u>Sound trumpets</u> for alarm, for assemblies, war, gladness, beginnings of months, and <u>appointed Feasts.</u>	Laws: X: 28–30, Daily offerings, beginnings of months, Sabbaths, <u>appointed feasts</u> (28): <u>sound trumpets,</u> 29.1.

Narrative:	Narrative:
V: 10.11, In the desert. Setting out from Sinai, the order of the host. Moses invites Hobab to guide them, 11. 11.1–3, People's first complaint punished by fire, second complaint, 11.4–13, wanting meat, 11.31–2, God sends quails. 11.33, the Lord smote people with plague. Seventy elders filled with God's spirit, and prophesy. Joshua worried. 12, Miriam and Aaron challenge Moses' authority. 13, Moses sends twelve spies to see the land, their evil report. 14, People complain to Moses and refuse to go on, Joshua and Caleb loyal. Moses confronts God. People repent but try to go up by themselves. Amelekites drive them back to Hormah.	IX: 20–27, Arrived in Kadesh, Miriam dies. People complain of no water, God gives Moses water out of the rock at Meribah. Edom refuses to give Israel passage. Death of Aaron on Mount Hormah. 21, Israel fights and destroys Canaanite King at Hormah. 21, Israel's victory over Amorites, Ammonites, and king of Bashan. 22–24, Balaam, the foreign prophet filled with God's spirit, prophesies in God's words, blesses Israel. 25, In Shittim people committed harlotry with the women of Moab and bowed down to their gods. Balaam blamed. Zimri and Cozbi slain by Phinehas. God's covenant of everlasting priesthood for sons of Phinehas. 26, New census in the plains of Moab. Levites in separate count, no inheritance.
Laws:	Laws:
VI: 15, Priestly perquisites, law of drink and cereal accompaniments of animal offerings, portions reserved for the priest. One law for the congregation and for the stranger; sinning through ignorance shall be atoned, forgiven. Man breaking the Sabbath stoned. Border of blue.	VIII: 18–19, Instructions to priests and Levites; priestly perquisites from specified offerings; tithes for the Levites. Levites' subordination reaffirmed. 8–21, Heave offerings and things reserved from the fire shall be the priests to eat in the most holy place.

Box 2. Defining the narrative sections.

The opening words of the narrative sections give the "who," "when," and "where" orientations.

Sections I and VII make a vertical split down the middle of Fig. 9.

Section I, ch. 1.1–2: "The Lord spoke to Moses in the Wilderness of Sinai, in the tent of meeting, on the first day of the second month, in the second year after they had come out of the land of Egypt, saying: Take a census of all the congregation of the people of Israel . . ."

Section VII, ch. 16.1–2: "Now Korah the son of Izhar, son of Kohath, son of Levi, and Dathan and Abiram, the sons of Eliah, On, the son of Peleth, sons of Reuben, took men and they rose up before Moses."

Now observe the "when," "where," and "who" statements that start sections III and XI, V, and IX, composing the two story rungs that cut across the middle of the diagram:

First Story Rung

Section III, ch. 7.1–2: "On the day when Moses had finished setting up the tabernacle and had anointed and consecrated the altar with all its utensils, the leaders of Israel, the heads of their fathers' houses, the leaders of the tribes, who were over those who were numbered, offered and brought their offerings before the Lord."

Section XI, ch. 31: "The Lord said to Moses, Avenge the people of Israel on the Midianites . . ."

Second Story Rung

Section V, ch. 10.11: "In the second year, in the second month, on the twentieth day of the month, the cloud was taken up from over the tabernacle of the testimony, and the people of Israel set out by stages from the wilderness of Sinai."

Section IX, ch. 20.1: "And the people of Israel, the whole congregation, came into the wilderness of Zin in the first month, and the people stayed in Kadesh."

The challenge for the modern reader is to discover what the two cases have in common: the innocent woman who is suspected by her jealous husband, and the man who has been defiled through no fault of his own. They are each put through a ritual that will enable them to go on with their lives. In her case there is no evidence of sin; in his case there was no possibility of avoiding the accidental defilement. The connection is not explained until we look across the diagram to read the matching section. In section XII, in the last part of chapter 35, we are given the laws on breaking the law accidentally. This makes the match for chapter 5, the woman wrongly suspected of adultery, and for chapter 6, the Nazirite who was defiled by accident: they are both matched by the long disquisition on the law of murder. In this chapter the prime issue is to know whether it is a deliberate murder or an unintended manslaughter. If the former is the case, the kin of the victim will take blood vengeance, but if it is manslaughter the killer may take sanctuary in one of the six cities of refuge. The three chapters, 35, 5, and 6, share the theme of the "not guilty" plea. The suspected wife who may be innocent, the Nazirite who was defiled through no fault of his own, the manslayer who killed by accident — the three cases are taken out of the normal ritual and legal process and given protection. The interpretation that covers all these cases is that if it were not for these provisions the law might have been the cause of an injustice.

Section III tells of the setting out on the journey from Sinai; it is paired with Section XI, which complements it by a summary of the journey and a list of the stopping places.

The short sections IV and X both deal with the calendar and the blowing of trumpets. "On the day of your gladness also, and at your *appointed feasts*, and at the beginnings of your months, *you shall blow the trumpets*" (10.10). By itself the word *trumpets* might occur anywhere, but in fact the two Hebrew words for trumpets occur only in this rung of Numbers. The phrase "blow the trumpets" is more complex. When we come to the matching section on the other side of the central divide, there, in chapter 29 (see Fig. 9 for sections IV and X), after detailing the ritual calendar of appointed feasts, the key words ("blow trumpets" and "appointed feasts") are given again: "On the first day of the seventh month you shall have a holy convocation; you shall do no laborious work. It is a day for you to *blow the trumpets*" (29.1); "These you shall offer to the Lord at your *appointed feasts*" (29.39).

Normally, by themselves, the distribution of short phrases, be there ever so many of them, is not conclusive evidence of a match between the sections in which they occur. Some later editor might carelessly stick in the key words at random. But the combined three key phrases ("appointed feasts," "blow the trumpets," and "in the beginnings of your months," 10.10 and 28.11) that are repeated in the matched sections IV and X cannot be found anywhere else in the book.[6] They are a safe cue to the parallel.

Sections V and IX both recount episodes on the desert journey. In both the people complain to Moses about food and water. Both describe fighting with the Canaanites: in V the people of Israel are defeated at Hormah, in IX they inflict crushing defeats on the Canaanite kings, including a victory at Hormah. Both describe the working of God's spirit, how it fills Moses, then the seventy elders, and then the foreign seer, Balaam.

Like other ring compositions Numbers uses various markers and other cues to identify the separate sections. They all point to the same divisions of the text. Identifying the units of structure is too important to be left to uncertain indicators. The same caution applies to key themes. There is often some fairly clear thematic unity that holds the two sides of a rung together; as in the case just discussed, trumpets and appointed feasts relate to the ritual calendar where the paired sections, IV and X, could be read consecutively without the slightest jar. The same sort of smooth continuity marks the move across the divide between narrative sections.

For example, it is easy to see that a section that has two events featuring the people of Israel angering God by wishing they were back in Egypt is to be paired with another section telling a similar story. Sections V and IX are both narratives, and both describe the complaints about food and water made by the people of Israel on the march from Sinai to the Jordan. "We remember the fish we used to eat in Egypt freely; the cucumbers, and the melons, and the leeks, and the onions and the garlic" (11.5). The two sets of complaints do not literally repeat. The first two complaints, in chapter 11, are about lack of meat and the summer fruit and vegetables they used to have; the complaint in chapter 20 lists the orchard fruits. "Why have you made us come up out of Egypt, to bring us to this evil place? It is no place for grain, or figs, or vines, or pomegranates; and there is no water to drink" (20.5–6). The parallelism between the two episodes is clear, even though they are well separated from each other by other events. In the first case, God's response is harsh; he is angry, he punishes them with fire and plague, but he also sends them manna and quails to eat. In the second case he is benevolent; Moses draws water for them out of a rock. But they complained again, and he sent them fiery serpents (21.6), followed by the remedy. The great importance of these episodes is that they are structural markers, which tells us to be sure the mid-turn lies between them.

Sections VI and VIII deal with the offerings of cereal foods and some meats that are made to accompany major animal sacrifices, and they are allocated to the priests. It is not difficult to see these sections as a matching pair. Between them lies the mid-turn (deferred until my next chapter). It is common in ring compositions for the mid-turn to

55

be flanked by two sections that are nearly the same. The parallels before and after the mid-turn form a triad that helps the reader to recognize the significance of the piece in the middle.

Commentators who read the book of Numbers as a linear sequence are understandably puzzled to find repetitions. Some suggest charitably that the weary editor nodded. Others take repetition as an instance of the lack of organization in the book as a whole. Sometimes there is a justifiable misgiving about the semantic fit that the key words and other signals indicate should be there. We expect matching sections to be related by analogy, but the parallel is not always obvious. The reader who is puzzled can take it as a challenge to reflect further and to consider the seemingly obscure similarities the editors had in mind when they strung what we first see as two apparently dissimilar beads on the same rope.

We have observed that the opening lines provide an unreliable basis for identifying a new section. "On the other hand," Goodman says, "the endings are carefully worked out."[7] The clinching evidence of the patterning lies in the finely worked perorations of each section, legal or narrative. "In sections I, IX, and XII, the final peroration is a summation of the narrative passage immediately preceding it, and is often in itself a repetition or rephrasing of a formulaic passage (e.g., divine command, Moses' response, conclusion/confirmation of action), so that in the context of the whole section, it stands out clearly as a conclusion."[8] Particularly interesting is Goodman's idea that some of the sections have an overall chiastic structure that frames and prepares their own conclusion. "Before reaching the final passage (9.15–23), the reader has already received an implicit signal from the structure that the Section is drawing to a close. Or else it is signaled by means of an embedded message, such as a word or phrase repeated three (or more) times." He gives section V's short concluding piece (14.40–45) as an example:

> And they rose early in the morning, and went up to the hill country, saying "See, we are here, we will go up to the place which the Lord has promised for we have sinned."

But Moses said, "Why now are you transgressing the command of the Lord, for that will not succeed. Do not go up lest you be struck down before your enemies, for the Lord will not be with you." [Observe the repetitive play on "up" and "down."]

But they presumed to go up to the heights of the hill country, although neither the ark of the covenant of the Lord, nor Moses, departed out of the camp. Then the Amelekites and the Canaanites who dwelt in the hill country came down and defeated them and pursued them, even to Hormah.

Goodman describes this peroration as "characterized structurally by four pairs of couplets, two of which are arranged chiastically and are situated in between the other two to give the sense of the passage's lexical keys, 'rising' and 'falling.'" The first half (14.40–42) contains the root 'lh ("to go up") three times and begins with way-yaškimū, "they loaded up." In contrast the second half has the similar threefold semantic associations from: "and you shall fall . . . and they came down . . . and defeated them and pursued them."[9]

In general the narrative sections have long, repetitive perorations and do not rely on the last one or two lines to mark the endings. Law endings are marked by individual words or groups of words repeated several times.[10] Like paragraphing or "chapterization," the positioning of the twelve sections conforms to a clear organizing principle of alternation between law and narrative. If there were no other markers, this principle makes it perfectly clear when one section has ended and another started. Once the question of how to identify the sections is settled, we can trace their arrangement in parallels across the board, down to the mid-turn. There we can see the gathering together of all the threads, and then up to the ending, a chiastic pattern writ very large.

We have mastered the formal structure of the book of Numbers and its outside envelope. Now we want to know what is encased inside it. Already we have come far enough to see that ring composition is a rhetorical form specially suited for summation and reconciliation. When every element in the composition interacts with all the others and nothing is extraneous or unnecessary, everything contributes to embellish the pattern. A well-made ring, like the story of the creation of Adam in Genesis, or like the binding of Isaac, gives the snowflake effect; like Francis Thompson's "filigree petal" it compels admiration. The reader's expectation that it will be exhaustively coherent, however unrealistic, is a great motive for exploring the structure in detail.

So far, we have looked carefully at the structure of Numbers. Even without examining the mid-turn it was easy to show the book's meticulous ring construction. It is like a demonstration model. When we come to the mid-turn, the impression of a strongly dominant form is further enhanced, except for one unexpected gap.

I start by saying once more that a ring composition condenses the whole burden of its message into the mid-turn. What has been seen through straight linear reading has to be read again with a fresh eye for the message that is in the mid-turn. Numbers would be a superb object lesson — until the very end. There we find that the editor has not managed to link the central meaning systematically to the ending. In a sense this makes it even more an object lesson, since it demonstrates the problems that arise when the rules have not been followed.

If we ignore the literary conventions to which Numbers mostly conforms we see only a mixed bundle of laws and episodes from the heroic story of the people of Israel traveling from Egypt under Moses' direction. But if we read it synoptically, as it is constructed, if we read it along the lines instead of down, we see at least two strong political protests. One is about the Levites, the other about the Jose-phites. Thinking in analogies and writing in parallels do not bar polit-ical criticism. A structure of matched analogies can make satire as biting as you could want, dramatic and difficult to ignore. The brunt of it is lodged in the mid-turn. A mere child, used to the conventions, could not miss it.

An Israelite child listening to a recital of Numbers would be seen paying close attention to the opening chapters (1–4). She would note that this is a story section of the book because it starts with a place and a date, and one action follows another in narrative time. Knowing implicitly that stories unfold along an internal chronology, she would expect them to be signaled by time and place, and would also know that Divine Laws are eternal, for all times and places. So she would be listening knowingly to the alternating bands of story and law. The exposition will be her main clue to the later unraveling. Knowing that the denouement will not start until the middle she would be waiting eagerly for the mid-turn.

As the sage child harkens to the exposition (chapters 1–4), she would memorize the names of the *dramatis personae* and note the four social divisions revealed in the story of the first numbering, the tribes, the princes of Israel, the congregation, and the Levites. At the end of chapter 4 she would recognize that the introductory narrative section has come to an end because chapter 5 starts with the law of leprosy followed by another law about breaking faith with the Lord, and more laws.

She may have spotted the ABA chiasmus of the first two chapters, and she will notice that the Levites occupy the middle position, the central place in this section:

A (1.1–46) The numbering of twelve tribes by the named heads of houses, counting all who can go out to war (omitting the sons of Levi).

B (1.47–54) The Levites are not to be numbered; they receive a special commission to look after the tabernacle, the altar, and all the furnishings, and to pack and transport the whole on the journeys to come. They will camp around the tabernacle. Unlicensed approach will arouse God's wrath, and the intruder will die.

A″ (2.1–34) This is a return to the twelve tribes, commanding their positions in the camp; on the east, Judah with Issachar and Zebulun; on the south, Reuben, Simeon, and Gad; on the west, the sons of Joseph, Ephraim, and Manasseh, and Benjamin; on the north, Dan, Asher, and Napthali. The Levites are safe (or under control) in the middle of the camp.

Well used to geometric thinking, when the child gets to hearing the mid-turn of the whole book she will not be surprised to find that the Levites are there, in the middle of the story and in the midst of the strife. From hearing the first two chapters she will have concluded correctly that this is a book about the Levites. Why should they not be allowed to bear arms? Perhaps they cannot be trusted to be loyal. Later events at the mid-turn will endorse this suspicion.

In chapter 3 God presents the Levites to Aaron as a gift. They are his brethren; Aaron is a son of Levi too, but now they are all called to do the service of the cult for Aaron and his sons. There can be no doubt that for these other sons of Levi this is a downgrading. They are to possess no territory, to bear no arms, and to provide physical labor for the tabernacle, and the sons of Aaron will make the sacrifices and act as their overseers. It is a humiliation for the Levites. This having been made clear, the Levites are numbered, the three families being headed by the three sons of Levi, Gershon the eldest, Kohath the next, and Merari the youngest. The various services for the cult assigned to each of the Levite families in chapter 4 sound like a lot of hard physical labor. Make no mistake: it is menial work. They have become janitors for the temple. Thus ends the first narrative section.

The young listener may doze through the laws in chapters 5 and 6 and wake up when chapter 7 indicates a return to the narrative mode by saying: "On the day when Moses had finished . . ." In this chapter the leaders or heads of families make formal offerings to the tabernacle. Chapter 8 prescribes what has to be done for inaugurating the

Levites for their task and announces that the command has been fulfilled. In chapter 9 the Lord gives the law for the Passover. Halfway through chapter 9 (v. 15), the sequence reverts to the narrative mode; the people set out under their respective military standards, following their leaders. The discerning young reader, or listener, who suspects that trouble is brewing for the Levites finds that there are several troubles on the way, but the major revolt of the Levites is hidden in silence until the turning point. It belongs in the central place.

In Numbers the central place starts at chapter 16 and includes 17 (section VII in Fig. 9 in Chapter 4). This is where the congregation rebels against the authority of Moses and Aaron. All the disasters foreseen in the exposition come to pass. Each of the three groups that has been mentioned there now plays its fated role. So smooth is the transition from the prologue to the mid-turn that the story could be read straight on, without bothering with the intervening chapters. In chapter 16 we hear at once about a rebellion against Moses and Aaron. The ring leaders are Korah, the Levite of the Kohath family (who in the exposition came in for special mention and warning, 3.27 and 4.1–17), and the sons of Reuben. They are supported by 250 of the leaders of the congregation. The latter correspond to the captains, or princes, or heads of houses, who in the exposition did the numbering at the command of the Lord. Now they publicly defy Moses, accusing him of pride, self-serving, and failed leadership. It is a takeover bid, a challenge to Moses' authority, in clear defiance of God's command.

In riposte, Moses accuses the Levites. Recalling the exposition, where they were separated from the rest of Israel and accorded privileged service in the sanctuary, he asks: "Would you seek the priesthood also?" (ch. 16).

Korah assembled "all the congregation" against Moses and Aaron. This brings all three groups of the *dramatis personae* of the exposition into the action. The congregation of Israel figured at the beginning as the subject of the counting, and in the count of their first born (3.40–50). Now they are in revolt, led by the Levites and by 250 other leaders. As events unroll, three punishments fall, one upon each of the rebel groups who had been warned in the first four chapters. Korah himself is swallowed up in an earthquake with his men. Two hundred of the rebel leaders (captains, heads of houses) die by fire. So the Levites and the captains have had their due, but the congregation of Israel is still not cowed. Next day they bitterly revile Moses and Aaron for killing the people of the Lord (16.41). The punishment that falls on them for this blasphemy is the plague; 14,700 died.

The wrath of the Lord has come out; Moses has been justified most terribly, by plague, fire, and earthquake. But this is not the end. There is another loose thread to be tied in. Aaron's authority needs to be publicly legitimized. Chapter 16 is only half of the midpoint of a ring that started in chapters 1–4 with the counting of the different categories of people. In the other half chapter 17 goes back to the beginning, with the Lord demonstrating his election of Aaron and his sons to the priesthood.

The plague is still raging. As if intending Aaron to be justified by a dramatic intervention, Moses sends him in to wave his censer amongst the dying. He goes in, and the plague ends dramatically, but the congregation persists in defying Moses. God proposes a trial in which he will show who is in the right. All the twelve tribal leaders are to give their "rod" (in function a minor ruler's scepter) to Aaron to keep overnight in the tabernacle. In the morning they are shocked to find that the rod of Aaron has burst into blossom. With a wealth of parallels echoing the beginning, we read how the divine demonstration of Aaron's right to rule over them devastates the rebel Levites and the others who have sided with them. It really terrifies them like nothing before. They run to Moses and say: "Behold, we perish, we are undone, we are all undone. Everyone who comes near to the tabernacle of the Lord shall die!" (17.12).

This is a very curious wording for them to use, as there has so far been no mention of the tabernacle in the course of the rebellion. I suggest that the editor puts that phrase in their mouths so as to recall the warnings against unsanctioned entry to the tabernacle in the exposition (chs. 3 and 4). Note there that God's original warnings used the words "any one who comes near" and "shall die" or "shall be put to death." "You shall appoint Aaron and his sons, and if anyone else *comes near*, he shall be put to death" (3.10). "And when Aaron and his sons have finished covering the sanctuary and all the furnishing of the sanctuary, the camp sets out, after that the sons of Kohath shall come to carry these, but they must not touch the holy things, *lest they die*" (4.15). "Aaron and his sons shall appoint them each to his task, and to his burden, but they shall not go in to look upon the holy things even for a moment, *lest they die*" (4.17). (This was about the Kohathites, the kinsmen of Korah, the future rebel leader.)

The richness and tightness of the weft is as impressive as in any ring composition we are likely to read. The mid-turn of Numbers faithfully picks up the story of the exposition and responds to its predictions. It also relates to the ending, where the Levites will be mentioned again. The mid-turn has not explained what it means for the Levites not to be counted in the census with the people of Israel. This is left to the immediately following chapter 18. The Lord said to Aaron, "You shall have no inheritance in their land, neither shall you have any portion among them. I am your portion and inheritance among the people of Israel" (18.20).

When we get to the end of the book, after their rebellion, after the rebels have paid the penalty for their crimes, the Lord does not forget the responsibilities he has assumed on behalf of the Levites. He assigns to them generous tithes from the people, but they still need somewhere to live. Fittingly, this will be provided in the ending, in chapter 35.1–8. Partly because of its general convention that there must be no loose threads, ring composition is good at grand custodial gestures. Here, at the very end, the Levites who have caused so much trouble are allotted forty-eight cities, of which six are to be cities of refuge for unintended manslaughterers. Each city has pasture lands for their flocks, so that they can live in the Promised Land, even though they will have no tribal territory.

The Levites are one of the central themes. God has been good and forgiving to them, but Numbers makes one message clear. No Levite can aspire to the priesthood unless he is descended from Aaron. Numbers has put a non-negotiable barrier between priesthood and the other sons of Levi. This is what the book declares, and in the fifth century, when Numbers was getting its final revision, it was a hot political issue. Because of the way it is elaborated through the book and tied into the mid-turn we can assume that protecting the status of the Aaronite priests is the principal objective of the editors of Numbers. This would have been for good political reasons.

When a region is shaken up by major crises, it often happens that a renewal of spiritual energies is released. In the region of Israel the eighth century was the scene of massive change. Particularly with the rise of the Assyrian empire and the movement of Aramaic and Assyrian culture into Canaan, the destruction of the northern kingdom of Samaria and exile to Assyria, and Sennacherib's war against Judea, the upheavals were accompanied by the rise of new spiritual forces. The Jerusalem temple and its cult became the object of attack by reforming prophets. The priestly editors were inevitably aware of the criticism directed at their established practice. They had another cause to worry.

After the return to Jerusalem from exile, Ezra, the governor of the province of Yehud, that is, Judah, was the Persian king's representative. He had sometimes been criticized for being a puppet of Persia, and for having it close to his heart to please the Persian authorities. He believed it was better politically for Israel to be seen as a quite distinctive culture in the region and would have dreaded the possibility of Judah being amalgamated with or absorbed into Ephraim as one administrative unit. His claim to have restored to the people of Judah the "Law of Moses" has been respected through the ages. Here it is necessary to note that the laws he insisted on most strongly were not recorded in Leviticus and Numbers by the priestly editors. For one, he promoted the Levites above the priests; for another, he demanded that those who had married foreign wives should send them away, and their children. He said that to marry foreign women is against the Law of Moses. Such hostility to foreigners has no backing from the priestly work. It is not the same law as the law the priests were teaching.[1]

This must have been critical for the loyalty of the priestly editors.

They were open in their foreign relations. If they had been isolationist they would never have been able to build up Jerusalem as a rich international commercial center. They had for many generations been intermarrying with the other Levite families living abroad. Once Ezra launched the attack on foreign wives the Jerusalem priests would have become overnight a party in opposition. This would have made them a political threat and explains why Ezra replaced the priests with Levites for teaching the law. With this background we can understand why Numbers downgraded the Levites to the level of janitors and porters.

The priestly editors would have suffered insecurity in Ezra's regime. This accounts for two other political concerns that weighed with them. One concerned the sons of Joseph, located in Ephraim, now known as Samaria. In government circles they were regarded as national enemies — fair enough, for there were wars between Samaria and Judah. In spite of this, the priestly editors would have felt loyalty toward the early Samarian priesthood, partly because for generations the two sets of priestly families had been intermarrying. They worshipped the same God of Israel and learned the same Torah, but over the intervening centuries Samaria had become a great, rich, and powerful neighbor and, under Persian rule, a major political threat. The other (related) cause that drew the editors' sympathy was resistance to the hegemony of Judah.

These political agenda help to explain an oddity about the book of Numbers. The listing of the twelve tribes is repeated seven times. The book starts with Moses being told to make a census, "Count the children of Israel," that is, "Count the descendants of Jacob." Moses counts twelve tribes (chs. 1–4). Although the sons of Levi have been dropped, the number has been made up to twelve by splitting the house of Joseph. By slipping in Joseph's two sons as separate tribal leaders Joseph now counts as two tribes. Ephraim and Manasseh added to Benjamin bring the Josephite presence up to three out of twelve tribes, quite a formidable constituency. The census is formally taken again in chapter 26 when the new territories beyond the Jordan are being allotted to each tribe, in accordance with God's promise.

Each time the count results in twelve tribes, including Benjamin and Joseph's two sons. On four further occasions the names of the twelve tribes and their leaders are called out. One is the marching order, the twelve tribes listed in chapter 2. Another is the presentation of gifts to the tabernacle, which takes up the whole of chapter 7. The givers are twelve princes, no more nor less. The fact that each prince on behalf of his tribe gives exactly the same, down to the last spoon, suggests that the count itself, the full count of twelve tribes, is the important issue, not the inventories of identical items given twelve times. In chapter 10 the marching order of the twelve tribes is announced. In the listings of the twelve tribes I do not forget the presentation to Aaron of twelve rods, one from each tribe, including Levi. This occurs at the central place, chapter 17, the impressive climax that focuses on the major crisis in the narrative.

To keep listing these twelve names was a fairly clear reproach to Judah, who claimed to represent "all Israel" to the Persian authorities. Along with Judah, two of the Josephite tribes (Benjamin and Samaria) were still on the political scene in the restoration period and a source of diplomatic anxiety. (The other remaining descendants of Jacob listed in Numbers had by this time faded out for all practical purposes.) The choice of Joshua, a man of Manasseh, as Moses' successor (Numbers 27.18, 34.17) was also significant. To recall the kinship of a hostile neighbor would not make the book of Numbers popular reading in Jerusalem, the city of David. This combines to suggest that a rebuke to Judah is one of the political messages of the book. One can speculate that the priestly editors' message was discomfiting to Jerusalem readers who did not want to know about the other sons of Jacob in what had been the breakaway Northern Kingdom.

Ezra's xenophobic foreign policy was bound to have brought him into conflict with the priestly editors of the Pentateuch. They were on the losing side in national politics. They disagreed with the book of Judges on the hegemony of Judah among the tribes of Israel. The book of Judges strongly supports the leadership of Judah: in its first chapters it describes the conquest of Canaan and shows Judah victoriously leading the conquest, supported by Simeon, while the other sons of Jacob lag behind in obeying the Lord's command to clear out the Canaanites from the land. Judges is particularly hard on the sons of Joseph: it emphasizes that they failed to drive out the people of the land (Judges 1.22–26).[2] This is in contrast with Numbers. Whereas Judges attributes the capture of Hebron and Hormah to Judah, Numbers attributes these victories to all the Israelites under the leadership of Moses (Numbers 21.1–3). The editors of Numbers never defame the Josephites. Their deviant political view would have put them in a very difficult position.

They steadfastly composed their books according to their political views, but their writing was of no avail. At the time of the redaction the non-priestly Levites had evidently superseded the Aaronite lineage of priests in their teaching functions. The Levites never exercised the priests' sacrificial functions, but very soon we find that the priestly role of the sons of Aaron has faded out of the history of Israel, though they still occasionally played a diplomatic role.[3]

In other words, the distinctive teachings of the priestly school were overlooked, lost, wasted. The editors were scattered and some would have gone into exile, voluntary or not. That is the context I suggest for explaining the down-classing of the Levites at the beginning of Numbers and their dire punishment for challenging Aaron's authority in the middle. In this respect, the final redaction of the book is an anti-government protest made by the priests on their own behalf.[4] The background of submerged political conflict makes the endings of the book of Numbers all the more interesting.

Numbers has two endings, quite distinct. One I call the ending, or the first ending — that is, the group of concluding chapters 33.50 to chapter 35. This is a proper ending; the great promises to Abraham have been fulfilled and the land of Canaan is being distributed to the tribes that were numbered at the start. On this topic the ending unmistakably matches the chapters of the census, 1–4 in the exposition.

The ending also has a curious point of parallel with chapters 5 and 6 in section I. This is again a very appropriate link for a ring ending to make because it doubles the link with the start. Chapter 35.9–34 is a fine sermon on unintended sin. It justifies the creation of six cities of refuge for the manslayer who did not intend to kill. I discussed this in the previous chapter. We have seen that the section that is facing chapter 1 has been well chosen to develop that very theme with two more cases in which the law is stopped from doing harm to an innocent person: the wife who is charged with committing adultery, though there is no witness against her (5), and the Nazirite whose body has been defiled through no fault of his (6), two analogies of the involuntary manslayer who needs to be protected from the dead man's avengers. The cross-linkage made by the disquisition on intention may look somewhat contrived, but it is clear enough—all the better for the argument that the editors were deliberately making a ring structure (Fig. 10).

With such a regular ring, showing such conformity to the norms for ring composition, we would expect the mid-turn to match the exposition. Now is the time to notice that the mid-turn, though it takes on the postures of a conclusion, makes no specific reference to the text of the ending. Likewise, the ending makes no reference to the mid-turn. The mid-turn, as we saw, tells of the revolt of the Levites and their punishment. The ending, at section XII, does refer to the Levites, but it is as if the dramatic events of the mid-turn had never happened. This is like a hole in the weft. The ending does not forget that the Levites are not to possess any tribal territory: this it has learned from the exposition. Because they have no territory, forty-eight cities are duly assigned to them, with pastures for their flocks. It would be forcing the argument to take that to be a reference to the mid-turn. The text says nothing to imply that the Lord's gift of cities to the Levites counts as a noble forgiveness for their revolt at the mid-turn. This looks like a loose thread in this otherwise exemplary ring composition. When we remember how punctiliously the editors of Numbers have conformed to the overall pattern, and remembering also the dangers of their political situation, we can suspect some gap has been torn in the text.

We need this background when we come to the latch of Numbers. Normally the latch makes an additional tie with the opening phrases

EXPOSITION
Chs. 1–4 Census of arms-bearing men. Levites excluded from priesthood, warned against encroaching on the *Tabernacle*. Sons of Kohath in danger. Aaron to supervise Levites. Key word clusters: "their fathers' houses," "lest they die."

SECTION I
II: Ch. 5, key word cluster, "*Put lepers out of the camp*," 5, Rite for a suspected adulteress; 6, Nazirite's *unintended* corpse contact. (Matching ending).

ENDING Section XII
Ch. 33.50, key word cluster, "*Drive out the* Canaanites." 34, distribute the land by lot; 35, cities for Levites; unintended manslaughter. (Matching exposition and Section I).

MID-TURN:
Section VII, Chs. 16 and 17. Same actors as in exposition, the Captains, the Levites, the congregation of Israel. Revolt led by Korah, Levite of Kohath's family; deaths of the ring leaders, each group punished, by earthquake, fire, and plague. Miracle of flowering rod, Aaron vindicated. Key word cluster, "we die." (Matching exposition only).

Fig. 10. Numbers's center at the mid-turn.

and events. This time, the latch (chapter 36) does not make the conventional references to the mid-turn. It repeats the case that was newly introduced in chapter 27.1–11.

In the latch (chapter 36) Moses is consulted by the Josephites: "Then drew near the daughters of Zelophehad the son of Hepher, son of Gilead, son of Machir, son of Manasseh, from the families of Manasseh, the son of Joseph." They ask whether the daughters of Zelophehad, whose father died without male heirs, will lose their lands if they marry outside their tribe (36.1–4). If there are no sons, may the women be the heirs? Moses consulted the Lord, and received the following answer: "The tribe of the sons of Joseph is right. This is what the Lord commands concerning the daughters of Zelophehad. 'Let them marry whom they think best; only, they shall marry within the family of the tribe of their father. The inheritance of the people of Israel shall not be transferred from one tribe to another; for everyone of the people of Israel shall cleave to the inheritance of his fathers. And every daughter who possesses an inheritance in any tribe of the people of Israel shall be wife to one of the family of the tribe of her father, so that every one of the people of Israel may possess the inheritance of his fathers. So no inheritance shall be transferred from one tribe to another; for each of the tribes of the people of Israel shall cleave to its own inheritance'" (36.5–9). In this there is no direct connection with the exposition. Though the theme of tribal inheritance is not raised at all in the first four chapters, the promised inheritance for the people of Israel as a whole is a background assumption from Genesis and Exodus, and the exclusion of the Levites from the inheritance of land makes it explicit. The connection with the exposition is marked in this passage by making "father's house" a key word in the latch. The phrase "fathers' houses" occurs three times in the first verse, as if it had been stuck in there for a marker (36.1). The phrase recalls chapter 1, where it occurs conspicuously seventeen times (2, 4, 18, 20, 22 , 24, 26, 28, 30, 32, 34, 36, 38, 40, 42, 44, 45). In the exposition the people were numbered by "their fathers' houses," and now at the end, their right to inherit land from "their fathers" is vindicated by the Lord himself. The editor has added a clause in which Moses guarantees to the Josephites their permanent status as members of the tribes of Israel. He tacks it on the end of the book and uses the key word cluster to connect it. To make a structural link only by repeating the same word cluster and not to bother to find analogous laws or events strikes me as rather clumsy scissors-and-pasting, not Numbers' best style.

The peculiarities of the Numbers latch supports Graeme Auld's reasons for considering the last part of Numbers to be a late addition. He sees Numbers as bridging two worlds, the earlier world of Exodus and Leviticus, where the Levites barely figure at all, and the later world of Chronicles-Ezra-Nehemiah, where they figure prominently. On stylistic grounds he shows that the "final quarter of Numbers depended on later elements from Joshua depicting tribal relationships, which in turn had drawn on materials in Chronicles."[5] This is especially interesting because it predicates interference with the original text on different technical grounds, and from different political angles, from those I would have expected from government loyalists in the Ezra period. Here is some late insertion that emphatically defends the right of the Josephites to be included in the inheritance of the children of Israel. Who would do that? I assume someone sympathetic to the agenda of the priestly school.

Let us conclude with a return to the dismissive reception accorded to the book of Numbers, the idea that it is confused and disorderly. This seems to be a bias in the Christian readership. The early Jewish scholars have no complaints on these grounds. They were familiar with ring composition; writing in parallelisms was a strong Semitic tradition. Nothing about this rhetorical style needed to be explained to the later generations. Eventually the ring tradition lapsed, which accounts for the baffled European scholars seeing only incoherence.

The reception accorded to it by rabbinical commentaries combined detailed examination of the text with the pious veneration accorded to the books of Moses. The interpretation they offered was general, moralistic, uplifting. The book has, however, an anti-Judah and pro-Joseph bias that would have been unacceptable to the leadership at all times. I suggest that the book remained uninterpreted because its political agenda was both impracticable and unwelcome.

six

MODERN, NOT-QUITE RINGS

We have now examined a particularly fine example of antique ring composition. Numbers fits Roman Jakobson's definition of parallelism as "a system of steady correspondences."[1] With this example in mind, we can better review his idea that a faculty for creating or recognizing these correspondences lies inherent in the relation among language, grammar, and the brain. Such correspondences should enable us to answer our initial question: why is ring composition so widespread? If Jakobson is right, it is inevitably spread far around the world. We should expect parallelism and rings to rise up in any region, at any period.

Jakobson's idea implies an aesthetic theory about the satisfaction derived from the brain making images of itself at work and duplicating its own structure and activity. The brain works by building correspondences and recognizing them. Jakobson was writing as a linguist about this mental process of dividing and matching. His materials for studying analogy were necessarily verbal; his examples came from poetry, words, rhythms, and sounds. We can go on from the verbal medium to consider creation of parallels between and across the senses. Making divisions and seeing similarities, matching parts, like to like — this is the essence of creativity. The internal pressure to extend understanding by new analogies is evident all the time, for example, when we create visual poetry, compose music for marching or dancing, or identify similarities between bodily shape and landscape. We can hope that studying ring form will enable us to go beyond words in asking more about ring composition. The next step toward widening the question is to look for it in modern literature.

The seven rules for the construction of a ring that I presented in Chapter 3 are not arbitrary limitations on what an author may do. They are requirements for solving technical problems in turning the corner of a recital and returning to the start. The justification for the rules is to preserve the ring shape. But why preserve it? What is the attraction of returning to the start? This I shall have to consider at the end of this book.

Meanwhile, it is useful to discuss what it means for a poem or speech to be shaped in a ring. And this entails thinking about the shapes of literature in general. Length, for example: when is the poet satisfied that he has finished when he writes a short poem? How to stop is one of any author's (or painter's, or preacher's) problems. A mundane and practical point of view would argue that the individual artist is influenced by the viewers' expectations. It sounds like a market response, but it is more complex.

Henry James commented on the difficulty faced by the novelist who first tries to write for the theater. The playwright's task is largely controlled by the theatergoers' convenience and also that of the actors. The play must be confined in a time-space between the closing of the offices in the evening and the last suburban trains at night. Somehow the play must be shaped into chunks that do not put the players into impossible positions (like being in two places at once) and do give them time to change costumes. James intimated that the external discipline imposed on the playwright by these factors was salutary. In a similar fashion, the seven conventions for ring composition serve as an author's kit for achieving balance and proportion. An ending that has been prepared since the start, the right ending for a poem of that sort, adds to the coherence of the whole.

No definition of the meaning of a ring shape will be true for all civilizations.[2] There is no meaning for the idea of ring beyond that assigned in a particular time and place. The ring may be a metaphysical model of world order — the Zodiac, for example. The book of Numbers arranged in a twelve-part ring may stand for the revolving seasons of the year. There is no saying whether a closed ring serves a philosophy of closure and fixed endings, or whether the circle is seen as one of a cyclic series that always returns to the same place. The myth of eternal return can be taken to be comforting and stabilizing, or it can be seen as a frustratingly sinister trap. Alternatively, it is equally possible for every ending to be an opening on a new ring, a philosophy of renewal and regeneration.[3]

Jakobson's thesis suggests a self-generating set of conventions that, with local variations, the common structure of language causes to emerge of its own accord. The other hypothesis is that the ring is a peculiarly complex literary form that has been invented once and found so satisfying that it spreads by diffusion to different regions. Evidence does not support either thesis. The speculation about a self-generating system gains some support from new literary constructions that almost reach ring form without drawing on a prior tradition. My idea is simply that it starts with the wish to bring a text back to its beginning before closing it down. In the effort to make a fitting closure, elementary problems appear, to which there may only be a fixed number of solutions. This would explain why literary constructions of the same type keep reappearing all over the world.

One way to test and support the speculation would be to study some of the almost-ring constructions in modern writing. Certain genres lend themselves to it better than others. We could expect the detective story to exemplify ring form because it starts with a who-dunit question and must end by reverting to it with an answer. But to discover a corpse at the beginning and refer to it again at the end is not enough for the work to qualify as a ring. We need also to look out for a structure that is held together by a strongly marked central place, with an internal organization of parallel rungs, preferably alternating in character, the two series organized inversely.

Detective fiction is generally governed by a principle that by the time the conclusion is reached all the loose ends must be tidied up, nothing left unexplained, everything accounted for. You would think that this genre lends itself to ring composition because the requirement invites a step-by-step reconstruction of the crime at some point after the middle. Following this rule Agatha Christie has composed stories that almost conform to the ring form. But we have to be careful. Even these do not quite work out as well-contrived rings.

One that superficially looks like a ring turns out, for example, to be

Table 3. *Five Little Pigs* as a parallelism.

I Carla's enquiry, her projected marriage to John	II Interviews with five suspects	III Five suspects' letters		IV Concluding review and solution
	1	1	1	John appears
	2	2	2	
	3	3	3	
	4	4	4	
	5	5	5	

only a set of parallels. *Five Little Pigs* comes in four sets of five chapters (Table 3).[4] After the introduction the first five chapters introduce the plot and its main characters. A young woman, Carla, whose dead mother has been convicted sixteen years earlier of murdering her husband, engages Poirot to find out who really did it. Unless her mother's name is cleared Carla feels she can never marry without shame. The murder can only have been committed by one of five persons who were present (and are still living). In each of the second set of chapters Hercule Poirot interviews one of the suspects; he also asks each to send him a written record of what they can remember. Each of the third set of chapters consists of one of the letters written by the suspects, presented in the same order, one chapter for each. The last section also consists of five chapters in which Poirot uncovers the real murderer through discrepancies in the written reports.

The whole book has a macro-parallel structure. Twenty chapters have been meticulously matched in pairs, but there is no development; they deal with the same event every single time. No antique ring would be so monotonous. True that the ending joins up with the beginning, but actually it never left it. There is no mid-turn; the composition is not divided into two halves; everything is piled on to the ending; the ring concept is not realized. The structure is a strong device for controlling the plot, but it is too mechanical to count as one of Christie's best books, and it is not a ring.

What about another of her books, *The ABC Murders*?[5] The book starts out promisingly. Poirot receives a challenging letter announcing a series of murders that will defeat his ingenuity to solve. The letter is signed ABC. Another letter tells him the first murder will happen in Andover, then there is a murder there, and the ABC Railway guide is found beside the corpse. He hastens there to check details. Another letter arrives to tell him that the next murder will be in Bexhill, and indeed there is one, and the ABC book is found beside the corpse. The same happens again for the third murder at Churston. The fourth occurs at Doncaster. In a lot of rushing to and fro Poirot is accompanied by a group of supporters who are related to the victims. The mystery is finally solved, but the systematic first half of the story is followed erratically by reports from local people at the four different places and by diverse half-revealed thoughts in Poirot's mind. There is no systematic sequence of returns to the first series in inverted order, and no discernible mid-turn.

Julian Symons was generous with his endorsement on the cover: "A masterpiece of carefully concealed artifice." A really good ring composition hides the machinery of its construction. The structure in this case does show rather obviously and it tends to overwhelm the narrative.

In spite of the difficulties, detective fiction does provide interesting comparison with ring composition on two scores. First, its structure is very formal, like that of ring composition. Its rules can be extracted from the stories and justified by the requirements of the genre. Second, it has a good claim to being a genre, not just a method of construction, not just a formal scaffolding for the plot. It was originally based on ideals of deductive reasoning and scientific method. These ideals engender rules or conventions that make them realizable.

Thomas Narcejac introduces us to the history of the genre by going back to what the early practitioners said they were doing.[6] Austin Freeman, for instance, remarked that the writer of detective fiction could not focus too clearly on personalities, lest the scientific requirements be pushed into the background. The requirements of the genre produce "a static person, with no future, no development"; a person's role must be subject only to the development of the story according to the pre-agreed structure. Freeman's style is impersonal; his aims are clarity and precision. "If a person could evolve, it would be the end of the detective story."[7]

I once asked a successful English novelist, Margaret Drabble, whether she had ever thought of writing detective stories. She answered emphatically "No," and, modestly, that she would never even be capable of it because one would need to start at the end. While writing her own novels she never knew what her ending was going to be. The justice of her answer is confirmed by S. S. Van Dine's twenty rules for a detective story as given by Narcejac (Table 4). Van Dines sees the reader and the writer pitted against each other in a gentle contest, parallel to the competition between the detective and the criminal in the story. Reading it is like a game.

The rules provide something like a golf handicap, an effort to make a level playing field or, you could say, an attempt to protect the reader from an unscrupulous opponent, the writer. They also protect the game itself. When we reflect on them, we can recall authors who have defied them, with deplorable results for the story. Unforgivable, outrageous, the author's tricks are crimes committed against the naive reader who believes that he has a fair chance. Like all cheating they are self-defeating because they spoil the game. The rule for fair play makes the game a very appealing analogy. It is difficult to apply such a rule to ring composition, which in no way resembles a competitive game, not even like drawing-room Scrabble. There is no occasion for competition. All the restraints on free composition are devised to resolve one problem: how to turn a ring. The decision to lead the text back to the beginning and to do it elegantly, this is the source of the conventions that have grown up around ring composition. For this reason, when I scan modern works for ring form I should ensure that the initial determination to return to the beginning is at work.

Before reading Van Dine's twenty rules, I thought that my first list of ten for the construction of a ring was too long. I cut down my list of indispensable rules to seven. At that point the ring form still seemed to be very restrictive. I thought it might be a problem to be addressed.

Table 4. Van Dine's twenty rules.

1. Reader and the detective must have equal chances of resolving the problem.
2. The author has no right to use against the reader any tricks or strategies other than those which the guilty party uses against the detective.
3. The true detective story must be free of any amorous intrigue. It must not disturb the mechanism of the purely intellectual problem.
4. The guilty party must never turn out to be the detective himself or a member of the police.
5. The guilty one may only be discovered by a series of deductions, never by accident or spontaneous confession.
6. The detective must resolve the problem through the signs revealed in the first chapter.
7. There is no such thing as a detective story without a corpse.
8. The detecting problem must be resolved by strictly realist means (no clairvoyance).
9. There can only be one detective.
10. The guilty party can only be someone who plays a significant role in the story.
11. The guilty party must never be one of the domestic staff, valet, cook, or others. The criminal must be someone who is worth the trouble of detection.
12. There can only be one guilty party.
13. Secret societies and mafias have no place in the detective story. It would merge with the spy story or adventure story.
14. The crime must be rational.
15. The conclusion must be visible all the length of the story, if the reader were only clever enough to see it. He ought to be able to guess the solution before reaching the last chapter.
16. No long descriptive passages or subtle preoccupations with atmosphere, they would burden the task of presenting the crime and finding the guilty party, and slow up the action.
17. The guilty party must not be a professional criminal.
18. The crime can't turn out to have been an accident.
19. Motive must be strictly personal.
20. Here follows a list of unpardonable tricks, ways of circumventing the above rules.

From Thomas Narcejac, *Une machine à lire: Le roman policier* (Paris: Denoël/Gonthier, 1975), 97ff. (author's translation from the French).

How can the authors of ring compositions bear to submit to so much regulation? But now, comparing the seven to the twenty conventions for detective fiction I realize that the ring composer is relatively free. The detective story is severely restricted; the rules maintain the genre and so provide the composers with a challenge and free space for creativity. Breaches of the rules are made all the time, and I do agree, as a reader, that the laxity is a form of cheating that does not improve the story.

I have no example as yet of detective fiction that conforms exactly to the rules for ring structures. But this digression on the rules of detective fiction convinces me that there is no reason why there should not be one. Some detective stories are structurally nowhere near rings, some are almost rings, and there may well be true ring forms to be found.

I will now turn to a very different modern piece that may perhaps be accounted as a ring variant, because the author clearly says that he is aiming at a return to the start. Laurence Sterne's book *Tristram Shandy* is considered by many critics to be the greatest English novel.[8] At the same time, it is said to lack structure. Great and unstructured, it seems thus worthy to be compared to the book of Numbers and the other works named in Chapter 2 for being judged disorderly and chaotic. In each case discussed in that chapter a hidden ring was there to be discovered, and I wondered whether this is true also of *Tristram Shandy*. I have reexamined it with the seven rules in mind, also remembering the implications of Jakobson's thesis that parallelism may crop up anywhere. Now, after the exercise, I have stopped doubting. I believe that it almost is a well-made ring. This case becomes a question of whether the author could have achieved anything so complex unintentionally, or whether he knew very well how to organize a chiastic structure for his long novel.

Commentators on *Tristram Shandy* vary between those saying that its true glory is in having no structure (we have heard that before) and others who suggest a structure of a musical or spiraling kind. "*Tristram Shandy*, in other words, like a piece of music, is marked by a kind of concentric involution, a structure — to change the shape of the metaphor, like that of a Chinese box."[9] "Concentricity, the spiralling pattern of graduated replication and varied repetition, is another such formal pattern."[10]

Trying to see how these effects are achieved will help us to reflect on Jakobson's meaning. *Tristram Shandy* earns its reputation for disorder by reason of endless digressions from any theme. The sense of spiraling circles is conveyed by moving away from a theme and continually coming back to it. Long philosophical disquisitions, short episodes and stories, personal opinions and encounters quite outnumber the chapters on the narrative themes. Sterne himself cheerfully admitted his many digressions. They take up most of the space, and the story of Shandy's life is swamped. It is like the problem with reading Numbers: is it a book of laws interrupted by narratives? Or is it a story of the Hebrew people interrupted by laws? It could be a mistake to take the biographical narratives to be the main theme of *Tristram Shandy*. Turn our expectations around and we could believe that the scattered philosophy is the main work, and the narrative only a minor set of strings meant for holding the thing loosely together. It would then be like a Mannerist painting in which the frame has teasingly become more significant than the picture it surrounds, a kind of literary joke, a reversal of functions.

Sterne says that his digressions are progressive. He justifies them, glories in them, and tells us that they develop the book's intention. He does not regard them as a weakness of the composition. "Digressions, incontestably, are the sunshine — they are the life, the soul of reading. Take them out of this book for instance — you might as well take the book along with them" (5.22). It is up to us to decide whether this boast is justified.

In Sterne's day the absence of form was admired as the sign of true inspiration. This is somewhat in the way that incoherent glossolalia is respected as a sign of spirit possession in ecstatic cults. And in the same way, the Persian commentators cherished what they took to be the incoherence of the mystic Rumi, taking disorder for a sign of inspiration. Laurence Sterne worked hard on the representation of carefree abandon. In spite of this, I still concur with those who maintain *Tristram Shandy* is not disorderly. I perceive it as a complex structure, and a deliberately created one, at that.

Tristram Shandy is much more tightly and richly organized than the critics allow. The various themes make a well-organized pattern of analogies (like the thirteenth-century Chinese novels described in Chapter 1). It is unified by the intertwining of several themes, developed according to the principle of parallelism typical of ring structure.

The story centers on two eccentric brothers living in Yorkshire. The elder, Walter, is a retired merchant absorbed in ancient philosophy, astrology, and science. He is the father of Tristram, the narrator. Walter's pretentious learning and his naive superstition is one of the targets of Tristram's wit through the book. His brother, Tristram's uncle Toby, is a war veteran. Wounded in the siege of Namur in 1695 and invalided home, Toby develops a passionate interest in the subsequent course of the war. With the help of his batman, Corporal Trim, he constructs miniature replicas of the battle sites on the bowling green in his garden. It is well supplied with water that they turn into a canal, copying the canal around the fortifications of Dunkirk. In full army uniform they daily reenact each new campaign. This gives the first important analogy on which the story is built: on one hand, the war itself, its battles and sieges, and, on the other, the miming of the war among the toy fortifications on the bowling green.

Tristram Shandy is divided into two books. The first places great emphasis on his father's character, on the events around the birth of Tristram, and on the progress of the bowling green fortifications. The second book is strung on Toby's affair with Mrs. Wadman, a neighboring widow. While he is working on his fortifications she is spying on him through the hedge and maneuvering to capture his affections, another kind of warfare. At first Toby is too engrossed with his war games to notice; later he tries to elude her schemes. Toby keeps abreast of the news from Flanders's battle fields and reenacts it on his miniature stage, until the war comes to an end with the Peace of Utrecht in 1713. Once the order has gone out for the fortifications in Dunkirk to be demolished, Toby, grieving greatly, orders Trim to demolish his miniature fortifications. Having nothing else to do, he starts to succumb to the widow's wiles and falls in love with her. The courtship is described in terms of attack, defense, siege, and capitulation. So the narrative thread across the book concerns war in three analogies: real war, war games, and the wars of love. They surface intermittently across the whole book. They are the background to ever-recurring episodes of false starts, beginnings that come to naught, disappointments, and new beginnings.

Instead of a coherent argument or dominant plot, the book proceeds by offering one analogy after another. Body corresponds to city, bodily ills and strengths correspond to a city's fortifications, the front of a siege stands for the front of the face, the nose the center of the face, the groin at one time the vulnerable outworks of the city under military siege and at another time the vulnerable male organ. When the architectural terms are extended to both structures the words come into collision, continually verging on indecency, and never allowing one meaning to overmaster the others.

Sterne intertwines the two lexical registers all the time, the language of military fortifications and the language for human bodies. Uncle Toby hears the specialized military register in almost any word. When Walter, speaking of grammar, says that auxiliary verbs are important, Uncle Toby warmly agrees, praising the service that auxiliaries provide in battle. When Walter refers to the curtain around his wife's bed, Toby starts off about the "curtin" that joins two bastions in a rampart. A conversation about mending the bridge of the baby Tristram's nose is mistaken by Toby to refer to a drawbridge. In the course of the book several narratives present elaborate parallels between the nose, in the center of the face, and the groin in the center of the body. In the Oxford English Dictionary "groin" can mean the snout of a pig and is also a stone pier built for a harbor fortification. This word, *groin*, is in frequent use because the wound Uncle Toby received was in his own personal groin, which makes the analogies tumble over each other more boisterously than ever. Nobody but Toby and Corporal Trim knows exactly where the damage was done, and when Toby presents himself as a suitor, the Widow Wadman, who has heard the rumors, is understandably anxious to know whether he has been unmanned.

The glossary for military fortifications in my edition is very revealing. When Tristram's mother is about to give birth, his father, Walter, wants her to have a local scientific practitioner (a man) to attend her in labor. She wants to refuse. Uncle Toby, trying to defend his sister-in-law's preference for the licensed female midwife, is stuck for the right word. He wants to explain why modesty would stop her from allowing a man midwife to approach her . . . (left as a gap); the narrator considers that the rude word the old soldier wanted to avoid was "her back-side." But the modest fellow finds that "too bawdy." He hesitates, and never finishes his sentence, though the narrator thinks that if he had not been interrupted he would have said "her covered way." So we look up the glossary note on "covered way" and find it stiff with innuendo.

A covered way is "a space of ground level with the adjoining country, on the edge of the ditch, ranging quite round the half-moons, and other works without-side the ditch."[11] In this context it serves for an account of the buttocks. Someone scoffed, saying that babies are born from the front, not the back, but to mention the frontal approach would be even more repugnant for Uncle Toby's modesty. Uncle Toby is a virgin; his ignorance of women and sex is another regular butt for the merriment of readers.

The war in the Netherlands might be the analogy for the fight for the life of baby Tristram, or the scene of delivery in childbirth might be the analogy for the war. The sense of reality is strong; the military puns are never so distracting for us to forget that they are talking about the woman in childbed. But neither birth nor battle, still less the toy battlefield, is the root scene for which the others are metaphors.

Of some kinds of books one cannot ask, "What is it about?" This book is not about something external, it is about itself. Does this mean that its main object is to celebrate the craftsmanship that it displays? William Freedman was right to say that "*Tristram Shandy* is about the way it is told. Form and content are one and both are present."[12] The starts and stops, the interruptions and digressions are equally present in two ways, in the discombobulated construction and in its themes. The mutual mirroring between the manifold topics and the structure of the book is the literary magic that compels the reader's attention.

Interruptions occur throughout. They tend to make fun of Walter, the portentous elder brother, who is continually interrupted in the middle of his learned soliloquies. At the beginning of volume 7 the narrator declares that there is nothing that he abominates worse than to be interrupted in the middle of a story. We have heard this before, and indeed the very opening of the whole book is about an untimely interruption of business in hand. Just as Walter is trying dutifully to concentrate on his Saturday-night sexual routine, his wife distracts him by asking whether he has forgotten his other weekly duty, to wind the clock: "Good God! . . . Did ever woman, since the creation of the world, interrupt a man with such a silly question?"

This is the mere fabric of the novel. It will take another chapter to unravel the pattern of parallels and concordances into which the material is woven.

A pattern of alternating bands was one rhetorical device that the biblical ring makers used to mark off units of structure. We saw this in the alternation of law and narrative for the book of Numbers and will see it again in the chapters on the *Iliad* in the alternation of nights and days. In default of an alternating principle, Laurence Sterne relied entirely on parallelism to mark his units of structure in *Tristram Shandy*. This partly accounts for the frequent repetitions.

The next question about the structure is, do the swirling spirals of *Tristram Shandy* have anything in common with the construction of the book of Numbers? Or any connection with ring composition in general? The period of composition stretched between 1759 and 1767. Recall that Sterne was an Oxford man, he had graduated from Jesus College in 1737; he was in holy orders and a scholar. He surely knew the Bible model if only by hearing fellow clerics talk about Bishop Lowth's famous lectures on biblical poetry delivered in Oxford between 1741 and 1750.[1] He could quite conceivably have copied the chiastic model for his book.

Lowth described a chiastic pattern that marks the structure by parallels linking the beginning, the middle, and the end, so that there are normally three key points and strong correspondences between them. It places the main message at the middle, effectively making the first and last part of the composition into a frame, often very elaborate. The series of chapters running from the middle back to the beginning go in inverse order from, and in parallel with, the first series going the other way. I will show how closely the structure of *Tristram Shandy* conforms to the pattern described by Bishop Lowth. I do not think it is quite a coincidence.

The test of what I would regard as a well-turned ring composition is the middle, the summary that marks the turning point. *Tristram*

Shandy has no central place. Normally, as in the *Iliad*, the central place in the composition recapitulates the beginning and anticipates the end, thus marking unequivocally the way the book is to be read and its key analogies. To find the center the first task is to identify the units of text that have to be paired with each other in two series, the one descending from, the other ascending back to the beginning. As I see it, Sterne has used two formal devices for structuring the novel: one is to divide the work into two distinct "books," and the other is to use the constituent volumes as units of structure.

Unlike the book of Numbers or the *Iliad* there is no need to worry that later scribes may have organized the divisions of *Tristram Shandy*. Sterne wrote his own book. He himself would have deliberately chosen the way his chapters are grouped in volumes, all numbered, nine volumes in all, some of them very short. There seems to be no special reason for this arrangement, except to use the volumes as dividers of sections in a ring-like organization. If that is right, volume 5 would be the central place in the middle of nine volumes. This would be standard practice for seventeenth-century poetry, based on Pythagorean number theory.[2] If these volumes are the units of the ring construction, then on either side of the middle volume two strongly paired volumes would stand on either side, in parallel. They are the sign that there is a ring construction. They will closely correspond, each to the other, a triangular frame for the middle, starting the return to the beginning.

If volume 5 is the center, volumes 4 and 6 ought to correspond to each other as the parallels framing it. I try it out for *Tristram Shandy*. It doesn't work. There is no obvious parallelism between 4 and 6. So now I try the idea that the middle comprises not one but two volumes, 5 and 6, forming a big central place flanked by 4 and 7.

The result is positive: 4 and 7 are clearly marked as a pair. From here we can tentatively proceed on the assumption that the central place includes both volumes 5 and 6. We shall find that volumes 5 and 6 do perform some of the main function of a mid-turn by making the necessary cross-references to the first and the last volumes, and more. Evidently the book has structure and the units of organization are the

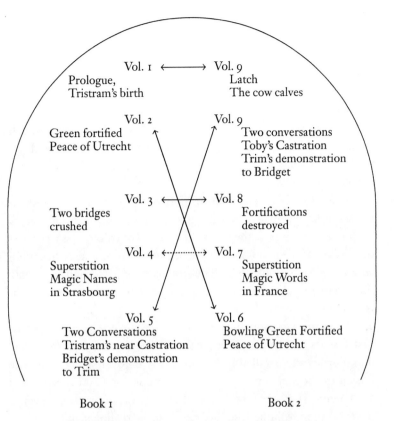

Fig. 11. Half a ring: The structure of *Tristram Shandy*.

volumes. That is already a result. We have established that it will be worthwhile to go further and test whether *Tristram Shandy* really exhibits a macro-ring form.

I am only half convinced. The book does not fulfill all the criteria that distinguish the antique ring forms I have been studying. If it is judged to be a ring similar in most details to the expanded chiasmus of the Bible, then one could suppose that Sterne consciously adapted it from the Bible. This is tempting, but I do not think it is the right conclusion to draw from the signs of literary structure (Fig. 11).

If it is only a nearly correct ring form, that suggests that it originated as a structure in the mind of the brilliant author, without his necessarily being aware of all the details of Hebrew poetic structures or meaning to adopt them. There is a lot of structure here, it is original, but it does not conform to any conventional formula. That being so, this book is an exemplar to support Roman Jakobson's idea of parallelism deep set in the brain itself.

The first of the two separate books of *Tristram Shandy* is mainly concerned with Tristram's father, Walter, and the second with his uncle, Toby. Our first act of analysis is to draw the line down the center.

Volume 1 is a like a classic exposition for the whole book. It sets the scene for the narrative in each half and introduces the main characters. Volumes 2–5 compose the first half. The end of volume 5 is written as the ending of the first book. At the beginning of volume 6 the author announces a new book. Volumes 6–9 constitute the second book, with the ending in 9. The narrator, Tristram, says in so many words that he is supposed to bring his theme back to the beginning (6.33).[3] This entitles us to try reading the second half as an inverted ordering of the first. It works out very well. When the volumes in the two parts are laid out in order, the parallelism becomes visible. Reading carefully with questions about the macro-structure in mind, we find that volume 5 and volume 6 both refer back several times to the information given in the exposition, volume 1, so the thing is properly linked up.

Given the many years over which the whole book was composed, the exposition was presumably written, as is often the case, after the ending had been done. Observe how it takes account of events on either side of the dividing middle line. Uncle Toby's wound in the groin receives attention in the exposition, though it is going to play a more important part in the second book. This also suggests that the final version was patched and rearranged for the sake of the unity of the whole. The process recalls the editorial work of Numbers and Leviticus, which assembled excerpts from very old texts. Ring composition is an excellent form for scissors-and-paste editing.

The most heavily emphasized links connect volume 2 with volume 6, and volume 5 with volume 9. It looks like a ring pattern with

Table 5. Three parallels between volumes 2 and 6.

Volume 2	Volume 6
New book	New book
Bowling green fortified	Bowling green fortified
Peace of Utrecht	Peace of Utrecht

the exposition standing outside. This double cross-linking is such an effective device for connecting what purported to be two separate books that I feel it cannot have just happened unintentionally. But the reader shall judge. The volumes 2 and 9 do not respond obviously to each other as parallels, nor do 5 and 6. Instead, 5 crosses the line between the two halves to reach forward with unequivocal parallels to 9, while 6 crosses the other way, reaching back to the beginning with stories that are paralleled in 2.

To assert a parallel with confidence there need to be at least two distinctive items found in both members of the pair, but nowhere else. Volumes 2 and 6 have it in common to be the start of a new book. There are three parallels between 2 and 6 (Table 5).

In volume 2.1–6 Toby and Trim thought up the idea of turning the bowling green into a toy fortification on which they could project the course of the war in the Netherlands (1692–1695). Volume 6.21 picks up the thread from volume 2 almost directly, by describing the house of Shandy Hall in Yorkshire, the garden and the bowling green, and the first two years of miniature fortifications.

The moment of transition in *Tristram Shandy* is the Peace of Utrecht, infamous in the eyes of Uncle Toby.[4] Reference to this important treaty connects the beginning to the end and the middle. The consequent demolition of Dunkirk mentioned at the beginning (2.7) is a crucial factor in the development of the narrative as it brings the games on the bowling green to an end in volume 6. This is where Uncle Toby hears of the perfidious order to demolish the fortifications in Flanders (there are delays and the actual demolition is not

Table 6. The three parallels between volumes 5 and 9.

Volume 5	Volume 9
Simultaneous conversations in study and kitchen	Simultaneous conversations in parlor and kitchen
Concern for Tristram's castration	Concern for Toby's castration
Bridget's hand gestures	Trim's hand gestures

reported until volume 8). We hear in volume 6 of Toby's deep chagrin and sense of betrayal after the Peace of Utrecht (1713).[5]

In volume 2.7 Uncle Toby mentions the Peace of Utrecht in connection with the shock he received in the affair with Widow Wadman. Volume 6 deals with the Peace of Utrecht and the order to demolish the fortifications and also with Widow Wadman's affair with Toby and his falling in love (Table 6). Both volumes 5 and 9 are endings. Three major links between them are as follows: two simultaneous conversations in kitchen and front room; two persons feared to have been castrated; and two hand gestures to demonstrate castration without indecent language.

The first of the two conversations, in volume 5, has Walter in his study, having heard of the death of his elder son, Bob. He is haranguing Uncle Toby with a series of profound aphorisms from the ancients on the theme of death (5.3–6). At the same time (5.7–10), Corporal Trim is haranguing the kitchen on the same theme. Then we have in volume 9.20–26 an argument in the kitchen between Bridget and Trim about Toby's wounded groin, while Toby and the widow are having a genteel discourse on the same thing upstairs in the parlor.

The second parallel starts when Susannah has held the baby Tristram in the open window to urinate, but the window sashes have been destroyed, and the window comes down with a crash on the child's penis (5.17). Susannah fears he has been castrated and runs to tell Corporal Trim. He then goes to describe the disaster to Uncle Toby by mime: "Trim by the help of his forefinger laid flat upon the table, and the edge of his hand striking across it at right angles, made shift to tell his story so that priests and virgins might have listened to it" (5.20).

The parallel is in volume 9.20–26. Toby declares his love and proposes marriage to Widow Wadman in the parlor, and they talk about the married state and the purpose of marriage as given in the *Book of Common Prayer*. Mrs. Wadman seems to digress; she asks obliquely whether the male member of her suitor is intact: "And whereabouts, dear sir, did you receive this sad blow?" (9.26). Toby circumvents the question by sending Trim to get the map of the citadel of Namur so that her curiosity can be fully satisfied. Returning with the map Trim first goes down to the kitchen to show it to Bridget. She has promised her employer to find out from Trim the truth about "that necessary organ," and Trim tries to explain the location of the wound by placing Bridget's hand on his own body, but she has information that the wound was more central than the manual demonstration implied. She contradicts him with her own manual display. Bridget is arguing (against Trim) that Toby has indeed suffered the equivalent of castration: " 'Come — come — ' said Bridget, holding the palm of her left hand parallel to the plane of the horizon, and sliding the fingers of the other over it, in a way which could not have been done had there been the least wart or protuberance" (9.28).

We learn later that Susannah, the maid in Walter's house, has told Bridget, and Bridget has told everyone in the village, and so everyone knows about Uncle Toby's mutilation. "In a word, not an old woman in the village or for five miles around, who did not understand the difficulties of my uncle Toby's siege, and what were the secret articles which had delayed the surrender" (9.32).

This is the end of the affair between Toby and Mrs. Wadman; their passion has been checked. For both of them it has been a frustration, a false start. The second half of the ring, which started out with her wiles to entrap him, is now well closed, and even linked to volume 2. These diagonal parallels, crossing over from volumes 2 to 6, and 5 to 9, systematically connect the two halves of *Tristram Shandy*. They show how much Sterne was concerned to make his work a unified whole in spite of the break down the middle and the wild digressions throughout.

Our next task is to demonstrate the kinds of correspondences that make the lateral connections. Bear in mind the fulfillment of these linking functions is one of the main reasons for the book's reputation for disconnectedness. And remember that we are not interested in thematic correspondences unless verbal indicators support them in both of the paired sections, and remember that it is word clusters that count, not isolated words. Following these principles, I find very strong parallels between 3 and 8, 4 and 7.

In volume 3 we hear the bad news of an accident to the miniature bridge over the waterworks in Toby's battleground. It is described as "crushed," "splintered all to pieces" (3.24, p. 171). Uncle Toby is very upset. Three chapters later in the same volume, we hear of the new-born baby Tristram having the bridge of his nose "crushed" (3.27, p. 174) by the clumsy forceps of Dr. Slop, who delivered him. So much for the man midwife Walter had selected for his scholarly credentials. When Uncle Toby hears that Dr. Slop is in the kitchen trying to make a new bridge, he assumes that the word alludes to his drawbridge.

Much of volume 3 is taken up with Walter's anguish over the disaster that has overtaken his baby son. His science and ancient philosophy have taught him that a beautiful, long nose is necessary for a successful life and that a damaged nose invites disaster. He prides himself on coming from three generations of long noses. After the first shock he tries to learn more about noses, and collects a library on the subject. Knowing something about his learning, we can suspect it is a library of astrology and ancient magic. This is the first setback for the young Tristram. Whatever else is related in this volume, it is dominated by the two bridges, broken by carelessness and causing deep distress. In this volume there is mention of the demolition of Dunkirk (3.24).

There follows volume 4 with a long essay on noses and names. Right across the ring, pointing from volume 3 to volume 8.10, we

learn that not only the drawbridge but the whole of the toy fortifications on the bowling green are due to be destroyed. Although it starts
with the episode of Widow Wadman falling in love with Uncle Toby
(which is also mentioned in 3.24) , 8.10 reverts to the war in Europe.
Toby has just had news of the Peace of Utrecht. He shares the anger
of the soldiers who regarded the treaty as a dishonorable betrayal. In
his view a war should be fought until the enemy capitulates. Just as
Walter was anguished for the destruction of his son's nose, Toby was
anguished on learning of the order to demolish the fortifications at
Dunkirk. How can his war games possibly go on?

Eventually, in this volume, Corporal Trim, under orders from
Toby, duly replicates the historical events. Bitterly grieving, he de-
molishes all the model fortifications on the bowling green. That is the
end of the stories about the toy fortifications. "Dunkirk" and "fortifications" are a key word cluster linking volumes 3 and 8.

With all this on his mind Toby is unaffected by the attempts made
by the widow upon his feelings. There is a great deal in volume 8
about Widow Wadman, her passion for Toby, and her wiles to attract
his attention. And plenty about his complete unawareness, his inno-
cence and ignorance of womankind. Henceforth Toby has no military
fortifications to play with; he is at a loose end and starts to think about
love (8.18, p. 465). War and love are parallel themes: military terms
are used for the widow's maneuvers and for Toby's early resistance
and later for his reversal of roles when he proceeds to lay siege to her
feelings. Most of volume 4 is about Walter's obsession with names and
his dislike of the name of Tristram, and about his superstitions concerning noses. The theory of names has already been described in the
exposition. His deep pain at his baby son's disfigurement is soothed
when he thinks that by choosing the right name for the boy the
disaster can be corrected. The child shall be called Trismegistus,
the name will "bring all things to rights" (3.11). The name means
"Thrice the Greatest," a later designation of the Egyptian god Thoth,
the father and protector of all knowledge.[6] It is a typically magical
idea, smacking of his crazy learning, as superstitious as his theory
of noses.

At first there seems to be no connection between volume 4 and volume 7, the latter is such a total digression, but wait! In volume 4 we have already been reading about sojourning in France. In volume 7 the narrator, grown-up Tristram, is very ill, so he takes a holiday on the continent. From the start both volumes are linked by reference to foreign parts. Volume 4 had the curious tale of Slawkenbergius in Strasbourg, the man with an enormous nose. When we come to volume 7 we read another curious story, about two French nuns in a carriage, abandoned by their driver. Slawkenbergius's tale is frankly a digression, but it does have direct relevance to the matter in hand, noses. In volume 4 Walter's theory of noses is repeated and Walter plans to cancel the misfortune of the baby's broken nose and to save the fortunes of the family by bestowing on him a magically propitious name. In volume 7 the story about the nuns seems to stand alone; nothing connects it with the rest of the book at all. It seems a true digression that has no relevance to the paired volume 4, except for taking place in France.

But when we reread both stories, in volumes 4 and 7, with the structure of the book in mind, we recognize them as the "progressive digressions" that support the book's main movement. In volume 4 the two universities of Strasbourg are embroiled in a furious debate about whether the great nose is truly a nose, or a false nose made of paper. The Lutherans form the anti-nosarian group, denying that God could or would have made such a monstrously big nose. The Popish group are the nosarians; they insist that God could do whatever he wanted and that he did make this huge nose, and that it is a true nose. The blasphemous satire makes a devastating backdrop to theological controversies that arise throughout the story of Tristram Shandy. Far from a digression, volume 7 ridicules Walter's theories of noses and names expounded in volume 4. It is a joke against the French and a joke against religion.

The further clue that the two volumes are linked is that volume 4 mentions the Abbess of Quedlinburg leading a great procession in Strasbourg. There are no other abbesses in the whole of *Tristram*

Shandy except in volume 7. The Abbess of Andouillets, accompanied by a novice called Margarita, is on her way to find a cure for her ailments (7.20). Their carriage, drawn by two mules, is driven by a coachman who addresses them in colorful obscenities. At one point on the journey he stops for refreshment, abandoning his passengers. The mules go on a little way, then they stop, and nothing the passengers can do will make them move on again. Panic strikes as they imagine themselves at the mercy of brigands and rapists. Margarita tells the abbess that she knows two words that will force any horse, ass, or mule up a hill, but alas, the words are sinful to pronounce, they cannot even contemplate saying them. The abbess hits on a solution: the thing is to divide the words in half, repeating the first syllable and then repeating the second syllable. So they say: *bou, bou, bou,* 100 times, and then *ger, ger, ger,* 100 times. Then the same for the other word, they say *fou, fou, fou,* 100 times, followed by *ter, ter, ter,* 100 times. They have not sinned; they never actually said the bad words. The joke is based on the ambiguity of the French *bouger,* to stir, budge, move, with suggested allusion to *bougre* (bugger), and the indecency of *foutre,* to fuck. It must have been a successful strategy because, though the mules did not understand the words, we are told that the devil did, and he left the women in peace.

One might well ask, "What on earth is this story doing in this book? It seems to have nothing to do with anything." But if you accept that the book is constructed as a ring, the answer is that the story of the superstitious nuns is placed just here in order to match Walter's crazy science and the wild superstitions of volume 4. French Catholic superstitions outdo Walter's learned magicality and form the link between 4 and 7. Furthermore, the story gives scope for an eighteenth-century Protestant gibe against Catholic superstition.

I will also suggest that this episode is placed where it is because it focuses on the idea of interrupted speech and emphasizes the master analogy that lies at the center of the literary spiraling, thus giving unity to the book. The dominant metaphor may be sex interrupted, or equally well it may be interruption illustrated with anecdotes about sex. It is, as the narrator affirms, that the diversions and digressions promote the theme, they illuminate an essay on interruption. If we have to decide what this book is about, we could well say it is about the disorder of life, its incessant ups and downs and sundry misadventures. But as a topic that is really vacuous. There is not one theme, but many. I claim that the disarray is only superficial. This is a book with a crystalline structure. It is so skillfully contrived that, if it is about anything, it is about itself. The way it is written exemplifies what is written. Cut it at any point, the same pattern is there. Look at the ending, for example.

It is a surprise to find a book that was written in such distracting conditions over so many years, including sickness and good health, presented in such a strong, subtle, and consistent structure. Written in the racy style of Rabelais, with the weight of Erasmus's thought, and with the tolerance of Montaigne, its author was obviously set on greatness.[7] If someone so opportunistic as Sterne is going to give himself maximum scope to play with analogies and to achieve repletion by their intertwining, he would have had to invent something like a ring form.[8] Sterne is like Turner working away at his composition in the Royal Academy until the very last minute allowed for the day of *vernissage*. The symmetrical structure results from his will to perfect his attack on the vanity of learning. He had to pull together a book that had appeared in parts over many years and had already been set into two volumes. The structure that crosses over two endings and two beginnings would be an original invention, worthy of the author's creative mind. I do not believe that it imitates an antique ring.

This being said, Sterne's decisions about the ending become the more interesting. In effect, one ending is not enough. The first ending does everything required to close the narrative in a coherent and comprehensive sequence. The second is a latch, a little surprise that completes the tale at a wider and deeper level.

Uncle Toby's courtship of Widow Wadman occupies most of the second book, volumes 6–9. It was always phrased in terms of war, attack, defense, strategies, and sieges. It comes to its climax when

Toby, supported by Corporal Trim, both dressed in full regimentals, set out to declare love, respectively, to Mrs. Wadman and her maid, Bridget (see Chapter 6 above). Book 1 (vol. 2) had made a great point of Toby's ignorance of the female sex. At the end (book 2, vol. 9), he is nervous as they approach Mrs. Wadman's door. "Now my uncle did fear, and grievously, too: he knew not (as my father had reproach'd him) so much as the right end of a woman from the wrong" (9.3). The reader can see that the whole second half of *Tristram Shandy* has turned upon Tristram's uncle's lack of education in the matter.

At the beginning of the second volume there is a reference to "the shock Uncle Toby received in the affair of Mrs. Wadman" (2.7). The expression "shock" is justified when we get to the distressing events of volume 9. She tries to find out whether his wound at the siege of Namur damaged his genital organs, and he tries to satisfy her curiosity about where he received the wound by sending for the map of the battlefield. "The shock" is his realization that the true information about his castration and impotence, so far from being hidden from Mrs. Wadman, was common knowledge locally and in the villages around. Trim finally told him in three words. Toby had interpreted the lady's thousand sympathetic inquiries about his wound as signs of love; now he discovered they were reasons for rejecting his suit (9.31). Toby will never marry Mrs. Wadman; their mutual attraction has come to naught. This is the definitive ending of the story of Uncle Toby and the affair of Widow Wadman.

The negative conclusion rounds off the many reflections on conflict, hesitation, uncertainty, and frustration that have been scattered through the whole book. It has accomplished enough of the things that the ending of a ring is supposed to do, by way of recalling the beginning and intervening episodes. Yet Sterne is right not to have been satisfied. It would be a mistake to leave Uncle Toby despondent at the end. He is the readers' favorite character. So the story goes on, there is a latch.

When Walter hears of Uncle Toby's distress he is furious. He launches on a vitriolic lecture against Widow Wadman, denouncing womankind and lust as the source of all evil (9. 32). To give Walter the last word on sex makes a clever tie with the first chapter of the first volume, where Walter's interrupted sexual activity preceded the conception of Tristram. While his tirade is in full spate the servant, Obadiah, rushes in (another interruption) with news from the farm — the cow has calved! The cow had been so long in calf that it was feared that nothing was going to happen. She was suspected of a swollen belly, like a "false pregnancy"; alternatively the bull was being suspected of impotence. Now there were rejoicings at Shandy Hall; both bull and cow were vindicated, and the female sex in general.

Much as Sterne was fêted and much as this book was praised, there had always been critics who hotly criticized him for indecency, and not without provocation.[9] It would have been a cowardly concession to those critics if he had ended with Walter's diatribe against sex. Yet a hostile critic might complain that the story about the cow proving her fertility is not a worthy ending for a book with such high philosophic pretensions. The latch makes an analogy between animal sex and parturition and the deliveries of a cow and of Tristram's mother. Is that not indelicate? And is it not too trivial a tale for concluding so many sage philosophical reflections?

In response to the critic I would say that the connection of the latch with the beginning has unparalleled richness. The whole story started with Tristram's mother being obliged to lie in for the birth at Shandy Hall instead of, as she had wished, in London (vol. 1). Her marriage settlement had given her the right to a London medical specialist when she went into labor, on the one condition that she did not contrive a false pregnancy, a swelling of the belly, as an excuse to get to London. Unfortunately, before she conceived Tristram she had claimed to be with child and had persuaded her husband to take her to London to give birth, as was her right. But the journey was for nothing; she actually had a "false pregnancy." So that is exactly why, when later on she was really pregnant, she had to put up with the discomforts and risks of giving birth in rustic Yorkshire, to endure the grotesque male midwife, his clumsiness, and the breaking of the child's nose. The end of the whole book gives us a new version of the opening theme.

Perhaps Sterne recognized some incompatibility when he half-dismissed the incident as a "cock and bull story." "Cock" has phallic reference, and "bull" means a "blunder, or inadvertent contradiction of terms." Christopher Ricks's essay on "The Irish Bull" gives reason to believe that Sterne was fully aware of this meaning of "bull" and meant to end aptly with one more pun.[10] As much as the book is about philosophy and morals, it is also about laughter, life, and love. A bawdy latch befits the merry book.

Unraveling the structure of this book has been very worthwhile for my central project, not a digression at all. The cross-referencing is found to have been so careful, it suggests an overall structure that was pieced together gradually. The more the book grew, the more it would become unbalanced and wild, the more the author would have sought for ways of tying the two halves together. So he has an exposition that embraces both sides in its scope. Then he links the two book openings (2 and 6) with a long and elaborate parallelism and does the same for the two book endings (5 and 9). After that it is easy to involve the remaining volumes in the pattern by elaborating them as parallelisms. Finally, the latch is a brilliant ending; connected with volume 1 it makes what Bible scholars call an *inclusio*, a containing envelope for the whole book.

With all they have in common, we must note the differences between the ring shape of Numbers and this ring of Sterne's. The latter has no mid-turn section that highlights a crisis in the plot, no tangle of dilemmas is summarized here, no dangers to be evaded or problems to be solved. The turn is made more brusquely, and very decisively, by announcing that one book is ended and another is begun. It is a crude solution to the problem of working back to the beginning. The second difference is that there are no alternating bands across the design of the whole book. These two deviations from the ring shapes that I have observed suggest strongly that the structure of *Tristram Shandy* is the author's personal response to the challenge of writing in a ring.

If this is right, it explains the recurrence of ring shapes all over the globe in terms that support Jakobson's thesis. The brain works by making parallelisms. No other explanation is necessary. We should expect regional variations and variations over time. It is outside the scope of this study to start distinguishing the eastern Mediterranean ring structures from Persian or Indian kinds. Given the initial homing impulse, the project of making the ending meet the beginning (that is, given the wish to write in rings), we can expect that local variations will be strongly elaborated wherever literature is highly valued. Why authors choose to clip the end of their composition onto the beginning, divide the ring in half, and make the two sides respond to each other in parallel formation, or why they should choose to write in rings at all, is a deeper matter. Presumably, symmetry, balance, matched proportions, and repetition have just as much to do with the way the brain works as the structure of language and grammar.

Lighthearted and profound, mundane and transcendent, *Tristram Shandy* hits both poles of order and confusion at once. Interruption is not the meaning; it is a means, an instrument that keeps pointing to how the book has been made, and keeps drawing the whole book together in a laugh.

We have now done a lot of spadework on understanding what ring composition is and is not. It is time to apply it to unsolved problems. The next chapters will study Homer's *Iliad*.

For those who know and love the *Iliad*, this and the next chapter are going to be frustrating. In this book the concern has to be entirely with the construction, nothing about the beauty, humor, and emotional power of the story. By this narrow focus we discover that the *Iliad* adheres faithfully to the seven rules for ring composition, though admittedly this claim is controversial.

Many scholars would now agree that the *Iliad* is highly structured and that the form is annular. Over time there have been many suggestions about the overall structure, but no one scheme is generally accepted. This is the paradox in its reception. Some of its most ardent admirers used to deny that it has any overall structure at all. A text that is like the Bible in having been transmitted from ancient times by many voices and different scribes cannot be free of discrepancies and anomalies. In other words, in the eyes of these scholars it would be a waste of effort at this point in time to look for a consistent ring structure. Some have maintained that it is a loosely connected bunch of poems and stories, individually brilliant but separately composed and brought together in almost haphazard fashion. It seems too mechanical to apply the rules of ring composition to this most gloriously inventive, riotously varied, powerful poem. As I have found, and said earlier, such repudiations of structure are like signposts saying: "Here lies a hidden ring composition."

I do not have a lot of sympathy with the skeptics. In fact, I do not see one ring, but I do see two. The main ring organizes the whole temporal structure into a numerical pattern of groups of days. At the midpoint of the main ring there is a minor ring that is organized in parallels, night to night and day to day. It is possible that at some moment in history one ring was superimposed on, or inserted in, the other. I personally think that the elegance of two rings, one taking off from the mid-turn of the other, the first being a frame for the second, is just the kind of poetic contrivance that might be expected of Homer. But that is speculation. Here I am concerned with what we have before us now.

As to structure, there have always been skeptics, some of whom date back to antiquity, starting with Josephus, and working forward through the centuries to the present day. In the eighteenth century, John Myres wrote, "Homer's excellencies were being depreciated and misinterpreted by the stricter French classicists mainly on the ground of their anomalies and the difficulty of reconciling Homer's treatment of his subject with modern conceptions of what classical literature should be." He remarked that l'abbé d'Aubignac "as a lawyer, was sensible of the discrepancies and anomalies of the action" and deplored the "looseness" and "wayward construction" of the poems as they stood.[1] That judgment is already a familiar refrain in the reception of ring composition.

Several scholars have tried but failed to convince their colleagues to accept their version of the poem's structure. They usually lack some means of distinguishing the organization of the poem from its theme. Trying to recognize structure by the ordering of themes is bound to be highly subjective. A formal literary structure is not the same as the thematic structure. A formal structure is not based on contents; it is a set of empty frames or containers for the contents. There should be always some fittingness between contents and structure, like that between the rhyme and meter and the thematic content of a poem, but searching among the contents will never of itself reveal the structure.

One simple method is to start simply with a search for repeated formulae that make a pattern. It can start with words, rhymes, assonance, alliteration, and can show also in nonverbal markers, such as line endings, and punctuation marks, commas, full stops, or exclamation and question marks. Think of the poet having to pour a newly formed idea into bowls and jugs of different shapes, some of which are at hand in local conventions, and some of which have to be invented.

The conventional variation in poetic structures will be found to depend on the type of social event for which the poem is intended.

Dirges, military marches, funerals, and sermons need to meet distinctive public expectations. The more traditionally hallowed and public the occasion, the less freedom the poet enjoys, as for example the strictures that the Somali poets have to observe (Chapter 2 above). Intimate lullabies and love songs are not necessarily freer, because their form can only take up the residual space left by the conventions for public performance. The history of the local art forms will tell us what the conventions are. This mode of enquiry is very congenial to anthropologists because it locates the art form in the social events that call for it.

Some myths are recited to celebrate boys' initiations.[2] In another case the myth of creation is recited at the beginning of a new political period to affirm the relations between the different shrines of the community.[3] Oliver Taplin follows this clue when he goes beyond recording the phrases, words, and themes of a great myth and records the occasions when it is recited and any prevailing circumstances that may assist interpretation.[4] He considers the great length of the *Iliad* and the intricate and overlapping cross-references that hold the huge work together. He proposes accordingly that the *Iliad* is intended to be heard or read as a whole, and delivered to an audience who are familiar with the story, or at least with the style. He describes the sensitive reciprocal relations between the audience and the poem. I believe this method of using the social context to define the number of parts in the poem to be valid.

Taplin's next question is when and how such an audience, large enough and distinguished enough to support the bard's fame, will be gathered together for long enough to hear the whole recital of the *Iliad*. Presumably the parts of the poem would have been worked out to fit into the given temporal structure. A three-day festival would be needed to support this poem, so it would accordingly be divided into three parts, one for each day. He proceeds to look carefully at the openings and endings, and at cross-references between them, to identify the three parts.

Taplin's method and argument are in principle convincing, but when it comes to finding the precise points of the divisions between parts he lacks a criterion. Size is the principle that has given him a three-part poem; he continues to rely on size of the narrative events to identify the three parts. For example, he suggests (to me unconvincingly) that the middle of the poem identifies itself by recording the biggest and longest battle of the siege.

There is another snag. His analysis only takes account of a small minority of the days that are listed in the tale. Noting that "about three quarters of the days covered in the whole poem are lumped together in blocks in the opening and closing phases," he decides to ignore them. He seeks the structure by studying the days of action.[5] He arbitrarily concentrates his analysis of the shape of the *Iliad* on the eight days of actually narrated events. I doubt that it is justifiable to omit the long blocks of twelve or nine days that are listed. The group of twelve days when the gods are absent, also the nine days of plague, the twelve days after Hector died, the twelve days of Trojan mourning — that is an awful lot to ignore. If we follow Cedric Whitman's account, these very same blocks of days are essential elements in the *Iliad* structure of narrative time.[6]

Cedric Whitman's appreciation of Homer's structure has the distinction of not confounding form and content. His method is first to ascertain the form and then to find what meanings have been presented in it. The form, as he sees it, is a pattern of days, plausible enough. He proceeds to count all the days. Like Taplin, Whitman regards an eight-day period of action as the centerpiece of the whole poem. This period is designed as a set of symmetrical opposites; it begins with a quarrel and ends with a reconciliation. The two sections (introducing and concluding) that frame it are both arranged in blocks of days ordered in an interesting numerical pattern. The first block is grouped into a "geometric structure" based on "the magic numbers 3 and 9."[7]

In book 1, on the first day, Apollo's priest, Chryses, appeals to Agamemnon for the return of his daughter; the appeal is rudely refused. After this day follows the group of nine days of plague sent by Apollo in punishment for the insult to his priest; then the one day of the assembly called by Achilles, when he quarrels with Agamemnon, a day that includes the voyage of Odysseus sent to escort Chryses' daughter home. One, plus nine, plus one, that makes eleven days. On the twelfth day another separate block also comes to an end; the gods return after their twelve days' absence from Olympus. On this count the pattern of (1–9)–(1–12) brings book 1 to an end.

This time series is the introduction for the central story of the Trojan War, but the latter is presented over eight days, and they are organized on a different principle. They are not an undifferentiated block but a detailed series of specified, identifiable days alternating with identified nights. They form a second ring. It is the mid-turn of the first ring that I am calling the numerical ring. It is obviously so important that it needs a separate chapter.

Book 24, the last book in the whole poem, is the inverted, numerical match to the introductory block of book 1. Book 24 starts with the twelve-day period of Achilles' mourning for dead Patroclus. Then there is one day for King Priam's visit to Achilles' camp to ask for Hector's body and to convey it back to Troy. Nine days are allowed for the Trojans to gather wood for the funeral pyre and, lastly, one for the day of cremation and burial (24.665–67).[8] That makes (12–1)–(9–1) for the concluding series of blocks of days. They are arranged inversely to the order of the first group, (1–9)–(1–12). With the eight days in the middle Whitman makes of the whole numerical scheme a regular ABCBA structure: (1–9)–(1–12)–(8)–(12–1)–(9–1).[9] This is a purely formal structure. It posits nothing about the contents, the most abstract, empty pattern imaginable.

Whitman's insight about the macro-scheme expressed in a numerical pattern is dazzling. The two blocks of days from book 1 and book 24 (which Taplin discarded from his examination of the structure) function to complete an abstract model of the whole pattern, a numerical chiastic scheme. The beginning series is matched by the end series, and in the very middle there lies the story of the eight-day war. As the central eight days are arranged in another ring (to be demonstrated) it would be more accurate to show the whole structure as two rings, one taking off from the middle of the other. I repeat: the outer ring is a frame; the first half consists of blocks of numbered days, and the second ring in the middle is the story of the war, structured on nights as well as on separate days, after which the second half of the outer ring resumes and concludes with a parallel list of blocks of numbered days.

As to the matching of themes, it is well known that the themes of the introductory half-ring, book 1, make unmistakable analogies with the closing half-ring, book 24. In the first a father (Chryses) comes to the Greek commander to ask for the return of his child, Briseis. He is refused. In book 24, again a father (Priam) comes to the Achilles camp to ask for the return of his child's body. This time the request is granted. The beginning is conflict, the ending is reconciliation. It strengthens the case that Whitman uncovered the original divisions. For my discussion of the war I will use the patterns of days and nights as editorial divisions, and only use the editors' numbered "books" and lines for reference.

The count of groups of days in the numerical ring starts with the appearance of Apollo's old priest, Chryses, before the whole army in council (1.1–42). He brings a ransom and begs for his daughter to be returned. Against the advice of the whole assembly (1.22–24), Agamemnon roughly refuses the request and sends the old man away with insults. Chryses prays to Apollo to punish the Greeks. This is one day.

Then follows another homogeneous block of time in which no nights or particular days are mentioned. Nine days of plague are sent by Apollo in punishment for the offense to his priest, Chryses. The text says, "On the tenth day" (1.54). Presumably that would be the sum of the first day plus the nine days of plague, which is still raging. On this tenth day Achilles calls an assembly of the troops and demands an enquiry into the cause of the plague. The diviner, Calchas, finds Agamemnon's intransigence responsible. In the hope of getting Apollo to end the plague, Agamemnon is persuaded to give back the girl. Reluctantly he sends her home to her father's island escorted by Odysseus. (That would be the same tenth day.) Agamemnon compensates himself by taking Briseis, the girl Achilles had won in war. In anger Achilles withdraws his troops from the war against Troy.

The Greeks are now facing the Trojan army without their strongest fighter (1.100–412).

On arrival at Chryse, Odysseus makes sacrifice to Apollo, who then stops the plague (1.457); then follows feasting and singing all day long (1.474). They are still on the tenth day. Odysseus and his crew sleep on the island overnight (1.476) and take their boat back the next day. "When the young Dawn showed again with her rosy fingers, they put forth again to sea toward the wide camp of the Achaeans" (1.477). That will be the eleventh day.

On day 1 Thetis tells Achilles (1.23) that the gods left "last evening" for Ethiopia and that they will return after twelve days. In other words, their twelve days of absence started the day before the first day of the eleven days of the quarrel sequence. After Odysseus has returned from escorting Chryses' daughter on the eleventh day, we duly learn: "But when the twelfth dawn after this day appeared, the gods came back to Olympus" (1.493).

It has been carefully worked out. The gods were absent one day before the insult to Chryses, absent during the nine days' plague and absent for the day of quarrel between Achilles and Agamemnon. Zeus learned about it from Thetis on their first evening back (1.494–510). Our reckoning of these two distinct introductory periods confirms Cedric Whitman's calculation of a system of (1–9)–(1–12) days. The day of the gods' return after the eleventh day is a new start: this twelfth day is also the first day of the next series. As soon as the gods are back we are into the second ring. Now follows the central period of eight days of fighting. It is a new ring that serves as an oversized mid-turn for the numerical ring, but it also has its own strongly marked internal mid-turn (Fig. 12).

The eighth day of fighting marks the end of the mid-turn of the outer, numerical ring. After the eighth day the numerical system takes over, with the last two blocks of days. One is the set of twelve days for Achilles' mourning the death of Patroclus, in book 23. Then book 24 records one day for Priam's visit to Achilles and the return of Hector's body to Troy, followed by nine days of Trojan mourning, followed by one day for the burial. It makes a pattern of (12–1)–(9–1).

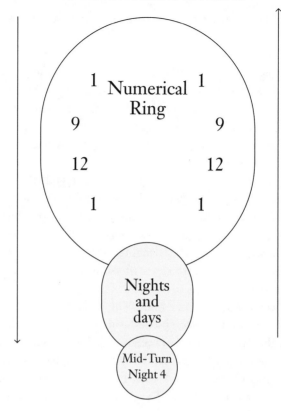

Fig. 12. Two mid-turns in Whitman's two-ring model.

Whitman's Numerical Ring

Bk. 1   The Quarrel (1–9–1 days)
Bk. 1   The Gods Abroad (12 days)
Bk. 23   Mourning for Patroclus (12 days)
Bk. 24   Mourning for Hector (1–9–1 days)

This is poetry by numbers, not at all the usual kind of ring structure. Instead of matching words and themes over two halves of the poem, the only matching that is done is according to the numbers of days and the sums thereof. It is clever, abstract, entirely formal, and peculiar.

At the center of the introductory and valedictory pieces is the mid-turn. It is normal practice in ring composition for the mid-turn to be arranged as a ring. We have seen that the mid-turn of the *Iliad* is so big that it dominates the whole poem prominently enough for some scholars to feel justified in leaving the surrounding frame out of account. This central ring is not a formal continuation of the numerical ring. It corresponds to the ring within a ring described by Otterlo, not a digression but an expansion. It is a set of nights and days organized by the principle of alternation. Counting them is difficult because the division by chapters distracts the eye, and yet it has to be done as it is also a numerical structure (Fig. 13).

In this ring the eight-day model of days and nights in the center of the numerical ring is exemplary. It is faithful to all the conventions. The mid-turn is the "central place"; it conforms to Alastair Fowler's analysis of the role of central place in seventeenth-century poetry.[10] All the meaning is to be found there. We saw in Chapter 3 above that the first basic rule is that the ending should be made to correspond to the beginning, and both should correspond to the mid-turn. To achieve this, the exposition or prologue must be designed to anticipate the mid-turn. The second convention is that the ending, when it joins up with the beginning, must make a clear closure while also using key words from the exposition and the first section. The third and fourth rules require a mid-turn that divides the composition into two. The mid-turn must be strongly marked. This is done by laying it between two clearly marked individual sections that match each other. They will be matched by content and by clusters of key words, one series looking toward the middle, the other looking back in inverse order. Lastly, the mid-turn corresponds to the exposition, using the same key words and repeating the themes announced there. Since by definition the ring ending must join the exposition, both the exposition and mid-turn refer to the ending, thus putting the whole piece into a tight corset.

The mid-turn is not in the middle in any quantitative sense. The best way to recognize it is by the two supporting series flanking it on either side and showing a conspicuous correspondence to each other.

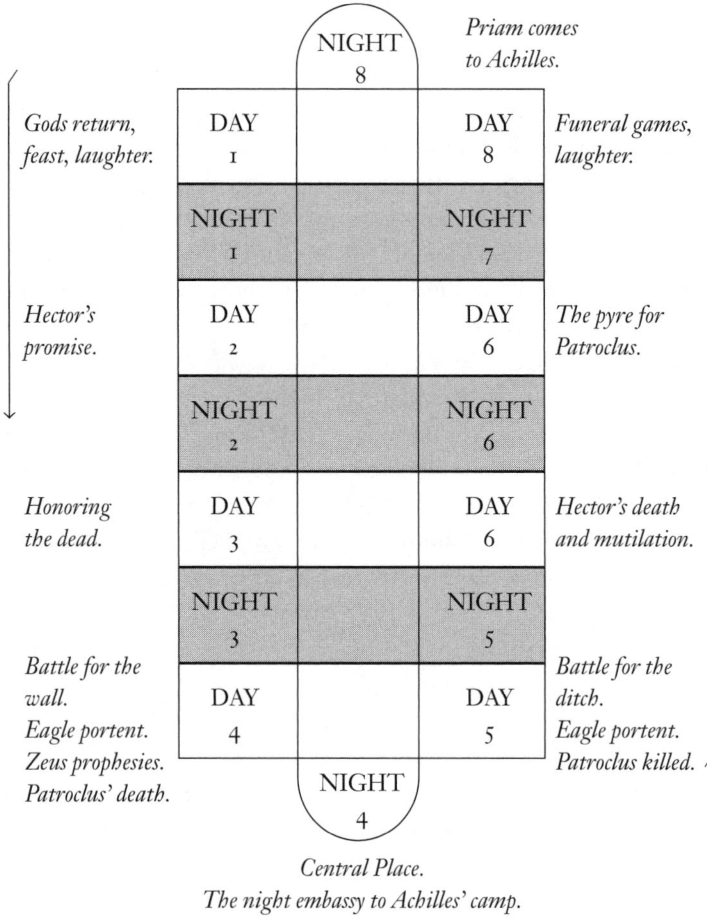

Central Place.
The night embassy to Achilles' camp.

Fig. 13. The *Iliad*: A pattern of days and nights.

In Numbers we saw that the mid-turn story of the violent punishment of the Levites' revolt is supported on either side by matching laws regulating offerings due to the priests and Levites. Here in the *Iliad* the events of the mid-turn at night 4 are supported on either side by the matching pair of battles. In the first battle raging through day 4 (8.1–485) the Trojans press the Greek invaders so hard that they are about to board the ships and set them on fire. A turn is marked by the very fact that the besiegers of Ilium suddenly find themselves besieged and on the defensive. In the second battle (11.1–18) victory of the Trojans seems imminent, so Achilles sends Patroclus into the fray, bearing his arms. Patroclus is killed by Hector. This will prove to be the real turning point, as it will bring Achilles himself into the fighting. The effect is to turn the mid-turn into a triangular three-part section, a chiasmus, ABA, another ring (Box 3).

Box 3. Dawns and nightfalls for eight days of war.

Day 1. 1.494, "But when the twelfth day after this day appeared, the gods . . . came back to Olympus"; 1.601, "Thus thereafter the whole day long until the sun went under they feasted in Olympus."

Night 1. 1.605, "when the light of the flaming sun went under they went away each one to sleep . . ." (in Olympus).

Day 2. 2.48, "Now the goddess Dawn drew close to tall Olympus with her message of light." The fighting begins, two truces, two single combats. This day continues to Book 7.

Night 2. 7.282–293, "Night darkens now . . . good to give way to the night time."

Day 3. 7.381, "Then at dawn Idaios went down to the hollow ships." Message to Greek camp, 7.420, "Now the sun of a new day struck." 7.433, "But when the dawn was not yet, but still the pallor of night's edge." Truce, both sides gathered in their dead.

Night 3. 7.465, "The sun went down . . . they took their supper"; 7.478, "all night long Zeus was threatening evil . . ."

Day 4. 8.1, "Dawn the yellow-robed scattered over all the earth." Great Battle; Zeus' eagle portent, Zeus foretells death of Patroclus, and entry of Achilles to war.

MID-TURN   *Night 4.* 8.485, "And now the shining light of the sun was dipped in the Ocean trailing black night." 8.500, "but the darkness came too soon . . . let us make ready our evening meal." Night embassy from Agamemnon to Achilles' camp.

Day 5. 11.1, "Now Dawn rose from her bed . . . to carry her light to men."
Great Battle, Zeus' Eagle portents, his prophecies of Day 4 fulfilled (Patroclus killed by Hector, 17.126).

Night 5. 18.239, "Now the lady Hera drove the unwilling weariless sun god to sink in the depth of the Ocean, and the sun went down."

Day 6. 19.1, "Now Dawn the yellow-robed arose from the river of Ocean to carry her light to men." 22.361, Battle; Achilles kills Hector.

Night 6. 23.55–58, "They got the dinner ready . . . eating, . . . they went away to sleep, each man in his own shelter." Dead Patroclus appears to Achilles, begging for burial.

Day 7. 23.109, "Dawn of the rose fingers showed on them." Funeral pyre for Patroclus.

Night 7. 23.154, "Now the light of the sun would have set on their lamentations." 23.159, "Bid them make ready their dinner." Greeks disperse to sleep. Achilles tends pyre all night.

Day 8. 23.226, "At that time when the dawn star passes across earth."
Achilles provides funeral games and prizes.

The *Iliad* aligns two series of days and nights on either side of night 4, day matching day, night matching night. They spread out from the center in obvious parallels.

There are five major cross-references from the mid-turn to the beginning and the end:

1. Bk. 9.1. The first reference to the beginning (Bk. 2) starts with Agamemnon's night speech inviting the men to go home, saying that he sees no hope of capturing Troy (9.16–29). This is a near replication of book 2, the first day of fighting, when Agamemnon tests the assembled troops with the same speech (2.109–141). The first time, Odysseus roused them to continue to wage war and they armed again. This time it is Diomedes and Nestor who rally the men.

2. The second return to the start refers directly to the quarrel: Agamemnon makes a formal apology for his injustice toward Achilles in book 1: "I will not deny it, I was mad, I will not deny it" (9.115–16). He then lists the vast wealth he promises to give to Achilles to persuade him to relent and return.

3. Third, the leaders decide to send envoys to Achilles that very night, to tell him of Agamemnon's repentance and persuade him to return. This involves reference to the initial quarrel. Phoenix, Aias, and Odysseus set out, they are well received and feasted at Achilles' camp. Odysseus tells Achilles that the Argive fleet will not be able to withstand the attack of the Trojans led by Hector (9.230–306) and begs him to return to the fray. Achilles refuses. Phoenix beseeches him again in a long speech.

4. Achilles' anger is not softened. This connects with the valedictory section, which actually refers to the anger which Achilles wreaks on the corpse of Hector, until the gods are disgusted and send under heavenly escort his old father, Priam, to stop him (Bk. 24).

5. Bk. 9.702. Back at the camp of Agamemnon the envoys' report describes the unassuaged anger of Achilles. This is the end of chapter 9. The night embassy fulfills the function of referring to the beginning by frequent references and connects it to the end by continual reference to the anger of Achilles.

So far, the mid-turn does exactly what it should do. But chapter 10 is not accommodated to the conventions. On the same night there are two spying expeditions, one team from the Argive camp, the other a spy sent out by Hector for the Trojans. It is the end of the fourth night, the end of the mid-turn. The recital here of an episode that does not contribute to the mid-turn's function is surprising in a poem that so meticulously follows the ring conventions.

The two supporting days on either side of the fourth night indicate their quite obvious parallelism. On day 4 the battle begins: "Now Dawn, the yellow robed scattered over the earth" (8.1). It continues all day. After great carnage "the darkness came too soon" (8.500). On day 5, "*Now Dawn rose from her bed . . .*" (11.1). At this point a new battle rages through seven more books, to book 18.235.

Two other parallelisms pair these two days (4 and 5). On day 4 Zeus sends up his eagle (8.247), which the Argives take to be a good portent for their armies, and Zeus also prophesies Patroclus's death and Achilles' entry into the war. On day 5 the eagle portent is repeated and the prophecies of day 4 come true. The supporting columns of the mid-turn have exactly fulfilled the rhetorical rules for a ring composition. After the mid-turn the fortunes of the war change direction, an example of mood change. It remains to look more closely at the two sequences of chapters that run on either side of the mid-turn.

The fundamental question keeps recurring. What sort of mental discipline does this literary form imply? From the list of rules one might suppose that it exerts a heavy-handed control. To be able to write in this exacting form might suggest a rigorous mental set in a strongly controlling culture. Is ring composition the tip of a psychological iceberg? Is it an example of the cultural control of creativity that the nineteenth-century anthropologists attributed to the remote peoples they called "primitive"? The *Iliad* is renowned as the most creative literary work of our Western civilization. The great advantage of being able to present it as a ring is that it gives a resounding answer, No!

Studying the construction of the *Iliad* suggests that the rules of ring composition are not like leg irons that constrain the poet's soaring spirit. Remember that Milton wrote *Paradise Lost* in exact mathematical proportions to celebrate the unity of knowledge and of creation. Being able to use such rules for poetry is a cultural achievement in itself; the amenities that the poet appropriates to realize the project. Moreover, instead of suppressing poetic invention, these rules stimulate and support it. And incidentally we discover that they are pliant — the thing can be patched and mended from time to time without anyone noticing, so long as the general structure is preserved.

We have noticed already that the most important technical problem for the composition in ring form is to demarcate clearly the units that are going to be placed in parallel with each other. For short poems it is enough to place a few key words to indicate the clues and responses, as in the Isaac story. Longer pieces face several technical problems. The beginning and ending of every section needs to be clearly marked so that there is no doubt about defining each one for matching the equivalent set on the other side of the virtual split down the middle. The reader has to discover what marking techniques the author used. When the marking methods are consistent through the piece, they endow it with unity and integrity.

The book of Numbers, as we saw in Chapter 4, marks its internal boundaries by alternating laws and narratives. Many traditions of alternation exist in the epic form — for example, alternate recitations in prose and poetry (called *prosimetrum*).[1] Male and female voices were alternated in the singing of Latin dirges. Even in modern detective stories, the narrative generally proceeds from two sides in alternation. Chapters that describe the events from the investigator's standpoint alternate with chapters describing the events in the suspects' lives. Not only does alternation mark the beginning and ending of equivalent sections, it unifies the piece with a common structure, creating overall balance and formal symmetry. And it relieves monotony.

Alternating bands across the whole book indicate both where one section ends and where to look on the other side of the ring for its equivalent matching section. The principle of alternation is a common method of marking sections for the large-scale ring composition. It almost makes key words superfluous, though repetitions of names, phrases, or events are also used to signal the parallel for each member of a pair of matching sections, and of course, the pairs that are matched verbally are also matched thematically.

No less an authority than Virgil himself revealed alternation to be his method for marking the division of the *Aeneid* into twelve volumes.[2] Three stories of action are separated on each side by two interludes (Table 7).

It has one exposition, a series of five volumes down one column, volume 7 at the mid-turn, five more volumes up the next column in inverse order paralleling the first, so that volume 12 meets volume 2. The rows are also divided horizontally by another principle, alternation of dark and light themes. To emphasize the resemblance between Virgil's alternating system and that of the book of Numbers, we can present it as in Figure 14, showing dark and light volumes in a pattern.

Table 7. Virgil's *Aeneid*, structured by alternating volumes.

I The Trojans arrive in Carthage, Juno raises a storm	
II Destruction of Troy	XII Rome's future assured
III Interlude, wandering	XI Interlude, truce
IV Tragedy of love	X Tragedy of war
V Interlude, games	IX Interlude, siege
VI Future revealed	VIII Birth of Rome
VII Trojans arrive in Italy, Juno raises war	

The excellence of the mid-turn of the *Iliad* is not enough by itself; we also need to take into account the series of parallelisms that cut across the poem's length. This is also excellently done. Once arrived at the account of the war Homer refines and tightens the structure by using nights for markers as well as groups of days. After the first numerical ring (the major ring according to Otterlo), the divisions within the eight days of war are marked by a precise sequence of sunrises and nightfalls. The attention that the poet pays to the first signs of dawn in the *Iliad* is famous, and he describes every nightfall, not so lyrically, but just as punctiliously. Various homely words, such as "time for supper," "feasting," "sleep," "darkness," "going back to the ships," give the signal for recognizing nighttime. The descent of night always followed by the arrival of "rosy-fingered dawn" gives alternating structural markers throughout the period of the war. So far the *Iliad* is exemplary.

But at this point my eulogy for the *Iliad*'s compliance with ring conventions must come to a pause. Homer has marked out the units of structure very clearly by alternating nights and days. We are entitled to expect thematic correspondences to slot into the places thus marked. This does happen insofar as the day is for fighting, the night for feasting, assemblies, and parleys. The days are bloodthirsty to a horrific degree; the battle lines are always shifting forward and back. Important things also happen at night, councils of war, spying, collecting the dead, succouring the wounded, and making decisions. Each day and each night moves the story along on the metonymic

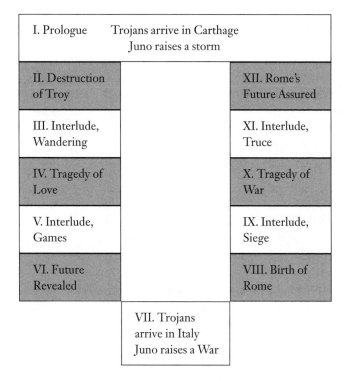

Fig. 14. The *Aeneid* in alternating volumes.

axis. But these diurnal/nocturnal activities are the only clear thematic concordances. A vast number of events are recorded for each day, but it is hard to make any other links between them on both sides of a matched pair of days.

Table 8 is regrettably overloaded because it has to present eight days and seven nights, together with the current book numbering and line numbering. With the alternating days and nights we have a pattern that is strikingly similar to the *Aeneid* pattern of light and dark themes, and also similar to the Numbers pattern of alternating narratives and laws. It seems to be a good start for our search for concordances across the eight days of fighting and their accompanying nights. But in practice only five unassailable correspondences show up. I have pointed them out in the previous chapter. There is the concordance between the exposition in book 1 and the mid-turn in books 8 and 9. Also note the correspondences between Achilles' unquenchable anger at the mid-turn and his conciliatory behavior at the end, books 23 and 24. Also note the parallel between the ending in book 24 and the beginning in book 1. Fourth, there is the clear concordance between the two battles placed at days 4 and 5 to support the mid-turn. Fifth, it is hardly forcing it to point out that day 1 and day 8 have in common feasting and the only mention of laughter.

This leaves us to account for weak concordances between days 2 and 7, and days 3 and 6. Their presumptive parallels are weak, barely recognizable. Day 2 and day 7 have in common only Hector's declaration that he will allow the corpse of any warrior he slays to be taken home, and his expectation that his own corpse will receive the same dignity (7.66–86), which makes an inverse match to Achilles' promise that Hector's body will be eaten by dogs (23.185). On day 3 the Greeks support the proposal to honor the dead, while on day 6 Hector repeats his oath of day 2 that he will honor the body of any warrior he slays. Ironically, he is killed, his body mutilated and carried back to Achilles' camp for further deep dishonor. Apart from these instances, much else happens in those four days that does not have any thematic parallels.

Admittedly I have scraped the barrel to find these matches. Days 1 and 8, 4 and 5 have already shown strong parallels, but all the other matches are based on the theme of corpse defilement. It might look as if they have been put in specifically as markers, except that they are scattered rather randomly. There is no other attempt to make the themes of the parallel days match each other. My best interpretation is that the structure of days and nights in the minor ring is nearly as formal as the structure of the groups of (1–9)–12–12–(1–9) days in the major ring, this in the sense of a purely formal structure being empty or independent of content. The poet's skill in this ring composition is to have produced two sets of four days, the last (Achilles' hospitality in honor of dead Patroclus) being brought to converge with and match the return of the gods on the first day. He has successfully made and closed a ring. That may be all there is to it.

Table 8. Big chart of the *Iliad*.

1.1–492, Achilles' quarrel and anger, nine days' plague. The gods' twelve-day absence.

Day 1 (1.493–611). The gods return. Achilles asks Thetis to influence Zeus against the Greeks. She relates story of the quarrel, persuades Zeus to side with Troy. Hera angry. Banqueting all day. Hephaestus jokes about his fall. Laughter in heaven.

Night 1 (1.605–2.47). Zeus sleepless, summons Dream (personified) to deliver a misleading message to Agamemnon.

Day 2 (2.48–7.293). Agamemnon proposes to abandon the campaign, hopeless without Achilles. Odysseus rallies troops. Army units marshaled, battle engaged. 3.85–460, truce for single combat, Paris and Menelaus. Paris rescued by Aphrodite (3.380). Agamemnon demands return of Helen and looted treasure. 4.105f., Pandarus breaks truce. Battle renewed. Bks. 5, 6, 7, Argives yield before Hector. 7.66–86, Hector will honor corpses of those he slays, demands honor for his own corpse. 7.67–282, Truce, single combat, Aias and Hector.

24, Achilles twelve days' mourning, desecrating Hector's corpse (24.1–140). Trojans' nine-day mourning for Hector (24.141–804).

Day 8 (23.226–895). The men return, wake Achilles, gather up bones, put them in an urn for burial. Funeral games, lavish prizes. Laughter on earth when Aias falls in the dung (23.784).

Night 7 (23.192–225). Achilles summons N and W Winds (personified) to blow on the fire, which then burns well. Achilles tends it all night, sleeps in the morning.

Day 7 (23.100–91). The Greeks collect firewood and stack the pyre for Patroclus. Aphrodite and Apollo protect the body from the sun and from dogs. In the evening the men are dismissed, friends remain, they light the pyre. Achilles sacrifices oxen, sheep, and twelve noble sons of Troy. He declares: Hector shall not be eaten by fire, but by wild dogs (23.185).

Table 8. *Continued*

Night 2 (7.293–381). Feast of the Greeks: agree to gather and burn the dead, build rampart, and ditch before the ships. Assembly of the Trojans (345). Idaeus dispatched to offer treasure and propose truce for burying the dead.

Night 6 (22). Dead Patroclus appears to Achilles in a dream, asking for burial. The Greeks take their evening meal and rest.

Day 3 (7.381–465). Idaeus delivers the messages. Offer to return the treasure accepted, suggestion of return of Helen rejected. Support for honorable treatment of the dead. Truce, both sides gather and burn their dead. Argives build rampart and ditch. Zeus and Poseidon comment negatively (445–64).

Day 6 (19). Hector imagines offering Helen and the treasure to the Greeks. Achilles receives arms, reconciled with Agamemnon (19.56). 20, 21, fights the river; harries Trojans. 22.66, Priam expects to be killed and eaten by dogs. Battle engaged, Achilles fights Hector, who repeats promise to honor body of the slain. 255–60. Hector is killed, Greeks mutilate and take his body, 330–404.

Night 3 (7.464–482). Both sides feasting all night long, while Zeus made thunder. They took the gift of sleep.

Night 5 (18). Trojans take their evening meal. Achaeans mourn Patroclus all night. Thetis commissions Hephaestus's arms for Achilles. Achilles will not bury Patroclus until he brings Hector's head.

Day 4 (8.1–485). First day of great battle. Trojans press hard on Argives. At midday Zeus sets his golden scales for Greek defeat (8.70). Hector drives his team irresistibly to the ships. Zeus sends eagle, a portent taken by Argives as sign of their victory (245–52). Zeus foretells death of Patroclus and return of Achilles to the fray (477–75).

Day 5 (11.1–Bk. 18). Second day of great battle. Second Eagle portent. Bk. 12, Argives driven back, Hector charges the ditch. Bk. 13, Third eagle portent. Bk. 14, Trojans cross the ditch, Argives in rout Bk. 15. Patroclus joins fight, is killed by Hector. Bk. 16, Hector about to burn the ships. Bk. 17 and to defile Patroclus's corpse, Aias drives him off (17.126–27).

Table 8. *Continued*

MID-TURN

Night 4 (8.485–Bk. 9, Bk. 10). "Now in the western ocean the shining sun dipped." Night council in the ships; the story of the quarrel rehearsed, Agamemnon admits his fault, decision to send envoys to request Achilles to fight with them. Night Embassy led by Odysseus as mediator, who recites the story of the quarrel with Agamemnon. Achilles replies with the story of the quarrel, rejects offer of gifts and return of Briseis; embassy reports back at camp. 10, two spying raids.

Here I must recall a precious lesson from Benjamin Harshav, professor of Hebrew poetry at Yale. I called on him for advice on the structure of the book of Numbers. I was worried about a passage that did not seem to fit the pattern I had discovered. He told me to cherish this piece of non-fit, love it, exhibit it, and never, never try to hide it. It is prime evidence of my honest search, and also evidence that I have not forced my own pattern upon the material. A smoothly perfect design would be suspect; a few mismatches in an ancient text that has survived so many generations would be much more convincing to discriminating readers.

Having laid this unforgettable advice to heart, I have suggestions for two problems about the structure of nights and days in the *Iliad*. The failure to find parallel themes filling all the formal parallels of days and nights may be turned to good account. The Homeric bards' performances would have been a creative interaction between the narrative traditions and their own poetic genius. There would have had to be room for including new developments. The strong framework of days and nights provides for just such available spaces. This would account for asymmetries on the two sides of the mid-turn. Furthermore, it would be no trouble to add an extra day and night, so long as another extra day and night are added at the same time to the other side of the mid-turn and some artificial parallel inserted into each.

There is a small problem about the number of days. I have assumed throughout that the period of war in the *Iliad* lasts eight days and seven nights. A well-known anomaly occurs in book 7 at day 3. The start of the day is announced at line 381, when the Trojan emissary, Idaios, rises at dawn to deliver a solemn message to the Greeks about a day's truce. When he has done this, he makes his way back to the Trojans, line 412, who immediately start to make preparations for retrieving and burning their dead. Then at lines 421–23, while both sides are engaged in this sad work, "the sun of a new day struck on the plough lands . . . rising out of the quiet water and the deep streams of the ocean to climb the sky." We get the definite impression that the sun has properly risen while they are working away. Is this another new day, or the same day?[3] Reasonably enough the commentators count it as the same day—that is, the same day 3 in my reckoning of days. But then at line 433 another new day is announced.

There has been no announcement of a night, but "when the dawn was not yet, but still the pallor of night's edge, a chosen body of the Achaians formed by the pyre" and built on it a defensive fort. Watching this building, the god Poseidon has a conversation with Zeus. This seems to be early morning still, but "as these two were talking thus together, the sun went down and the work of the Achaians was finished" (lines 464–65). This is presumably to be counted as the beginning of night 3. We seem to have had two dawns following each other with only one night. Everywhere else, in the whole book, every time a new day is announced, the following night is announced in due course. The system is perfectly consistent, except in this one place. Either it is all happening on the one day, between the first dawn and the sunset, or there were two dawns and no night in between. Perhaps it is ambiguous because the day's truce was not supposed to be spent on defense works. If that is the point, the Greeks are cheating on the truce as the Trojans did on day 2 (4.105 ff.). Or perhaps it is just a confusion due to poems' ancient and vulnerable process of transmission.

These mentions of dawn and day suggest that a night is missing between the inauguration of day 3 and the arrival of night 3, which is unambiguously announced by the words *"And then the sun went down"* (7.464). If there is a missing night and if we insert it, day 3 is split into two days, and night 3 becomes night 4, and so on, with the result that the eight-day period is now nine days. Adding a day would dislocate the pairing of parallel days across the middle of the ring, so I gratefully choose to follow the practice of ignoring the anomaly.

We have noted that Whitman makes of the whole numerical scheme a regular ABCBA structure with eight days of war in the middle: (1–9)–(1–12)–(8)–(12–1)–(9–1).[4] His numerical scheme is a regular ABCBA structure: (1–9)–(1–12)–(8)–(12–1)–(9–1).[5] This being a purely formal structure, it posits nothing about the contents. But now it strikes me that the (8) at the midpoint of his numerical ring is a bit of a disappointment. A pattern of 1's, 9's, and 12's might have been more satisfactory. It may be wild to suggest that there may have been an earlier version in which day 3 was split into two days. And another day added on the other side of the mid-turn. It is just a speculation inspired by the only anomaly in the count of days and in Whitman's model.

We have now examined the two sequences of chapters, one that runs from day 1 to night 4 and the other one that parallels it, going from day 5 to day 8. Unexpectedly, the same analysis that demonstrated that *Tristram Shandy* is almost, but not quite, in ring form and that unraveled the alleged confusion of the book of Numbers reveals that Homer and the editor of Numbers have used the same pattern of composition. The main difference is that the *Iliad*, adhering to the same rules, is more complex and more coherent. The *Iliad's* ending, mid-turn, and exposition match each other better. Though the pattern of alternating days and nights is not as unambiguous as the pattern of alternating narrative and law in Numbers, the poem does conform to the principal conditions for making a ring.

With all this held in mind, if I were to ask myself honestly whether I think the *Iliad* is or is not a well-formed ring, my own answer is positive. Yes. It is an excellent example of ring structure, but over the centuries there have been a few changes. In a work like this, so intricately organized, even a small change can disrupt the system of days, and subsequent scribes then have a hard task to set it right again. This is what seems to have happened here around the middle of the action. However, the crucial requirements are for parallels between the middle, the beginning, and the end. These the *Iliad* fully meets.

Arrived at this chapter we face several questions about endings. Our first will concern the way that actual rings come to their ending. This includes what the ending does for the composition, how it is done. That will be easy. More difficult is solving Jakobson's conundrum described in Chapter 1, which must be attempted if my ending is to meet my beginning.

The great philologist considered that parallelism is a faculty inherent in the relation among language, grammar, and the brain. Once the ring structure has been explained as a system of parallelisms, the puzzle takes a new turn. Why is it so difficult to recognize? It hardly seems plausible that the scholars balk at the circular system just because they are used to linear reading and writing. Roman Jakobson's theory that precisely this kind of analogic arrangement is deep wired into the human capacity for language becomes a paradox. Surely we should all be capable of appreciating a structure of parallelisms at first sight?

There are several unconvincing explanations. One is simple prejudice against foreigners: perhaps we read archaic literature with a concealed "Orientalist" contempt. Are we like the ancient Greeks in regard to anyone they called "barbarian"? Admittedly, the record does not suggest that we do expect "Oriental" writings, or oral literature, to be elegant or capable of effective expression, but nor do we seem to be specially prejudiced against them. A slightly more plausible explanation might be that it is a side effect of social Darwinism with its emphasis on moral and intellectual evolution. From this, combined with our colonial tradition, we learned that the so-called primitive peoples over whom we ruled were still at a childish stage of evolution, morally and intellectually, so we were never looking for literary sophistication.

These bequeathed ideas may have limited our capacity for appreciating other people's artistic refinement. Once it has been discarded as a method of literary construction, that is to say when there are no contemporary ring compositions being produced, it is understandable that it should be overlooked by the readers. When it goes out of fashion, it comes to an unlamented, unrecorded, end.

The writer who believes that a recognizable ending is necessary will have to decide when and how to end, whether to make it a triumphal justification of the original position, or a terrible warning, or whether a modest summary will serve. For the author composing a polished ring there is little choice; the ending is prescribed. The rules, which I have elicited by reading endings of rings, are three:

1. The ending must evoke the beginning; it should close the ring by touching on the topics that were opened by either the exposition, or the section following it, or both, using some of the same words.
2. To have followed the first rule automatically evokes the mid-turn, which has itself been designed to connect with the ending as well as with the beginning.
3. It may make a double closure, using the option of the "latch." In this case, the first ending will finish the immediate business, conclude the story, or round off the laws. The second ending will set the text as a whole in a larger context, less parochial, more humanist, or even metaphysical.

I pause here to ask why a poet should have the ambition to make a polished ring. Would not something rough and ready do? In my first chapter I described the context of recital and the function that a well-turned poem performs by way of authenticating the status of the bard. Professional performance always has an element of competition.[1] It is not just a matter of payment, or just a matter of gaining fame; there is the practical problem of the box office. A bard needs to draw an audience; the need puts him in tacit competition with the others. If he and his team can count on a large audience at the major feasts, they are winning. As he climbs the ladder of success he will encounter more and more discriminating audiences. In the triadic interaction between poet, audience, and poem the conventions will be continually sharpened. The pressure for quality encourages him to abide by the rules, refine them, and make the composition more complex.

Glenn Most considers that its complexity explains the difficulties that modern readers have in interpreting Pindar's poetry. He holds that "each poem of Pindar is organized systematically as an immanent compositional unity whose form can be interpreted as appropriate for its unique content. . . . 'Compositional form' depends on spatio-temporal concreteness of the art-work . . . the arrangement of the parts is neither capricious nor arbitrary—none of its parts can be substituted or exchanged against some part of another text . . . without the substitution being noticeable. The sequence is not random."[2]

He concludes that the unity of the poem derives from "the formal design whereby all the elements are integrated into a coherent totality, and the formal design itself is part of Pindar's meaning." The idea of the poet's formal design controlling the parts and conferring unity on the poem corresponds closely to the concept of repleteness in a work of art. The strength of this concept is that it comes so close to the way modern artists themselves talk about painting. Matisse, for example, had an idea of this kind in the forefront of his mind all the time. He was driven by the desire to realize his original vision of a painting as closely as possible. His advice to painters was: "When painting, first look long and well at your model or subject, and decide on your general colour scheme. This must prevail. In painting a landscape you choose it for certain beauties — spots of colour, suggestions of composition. Close your eyes and visualize the picture; then go to work, always keeping these characteristics the important features of your picture. And you must at once indicate all that you would have in the complete work. All must be considered in interrelation during the process — nothing can be added."[3]

Matisse repeated this advice, to strive for fidelity to an original vision, to lose nothing of it, and to add nothing, always with emphasis on the interrelation of the elements. On the process of making a painting he said, "I want to reach that state of condensation of sensations which makes a painting."

He accepted changes that take place as the picture is being re-worked, but the direction of this process of constant change is always back to the beginning: "For me all is in the conception. I must there-fore have a clear vision of the whole from the beginning."[4]

What he wanted to achieve is nothing more and nothing less than that original vision, and everything condensed around that point. Roger Fry is another modern painter who looked for a similar effect, what he called "that unity of feeling."[5]

Their shared idea of the finished painting corresponds closely to the philosopher's concept of repleteness. Nelson Goodman's episte-mology of rightness is helpful here.[6] In *Languages of Art* he directs our attention to "fittingness" and to the schemes of thought in which an element may be seen as right, and particularly to connoisseurship.[7] Because the latter, connoisseurship, is a key element in the situation of bardic performance and reception, a digression is in order.

Goodman takes judgments of beauty and value out of the range of misty universals and subjective sensibilities. His focus on "rightness of categories" extends Wittgenstein's concern with rule-following and with rightness as central aesthetic concepts. Both men take aesthetic judgment to be a matter of connoisseurship, knowing the scheme of ideas, knowing the well-made garment: "What does a per-son who knows a good suit say when trying on a suit at the tai-lor's? 'That's the right length,' 'That's too short,' 'That's too narrow.' Words of approval play no role, although he will look pleased when the coat suits him."[8]

On these lines, the preliminary work of the art historian is to find the right categories for placing particular works. Do the members assigned to the category fit it? It may come up as a matter of authen-tication ("Is this a genuine Rembrandt?"), or as a matter of correct classification ("Does this painting belong with the Mannerists?"). Or more profoundly, the art historians may be asking each other, "Have we got the right categories, knowing what is being attempted? Recall Wittgenstein's homely example of categories for our enquiry?"

For answering such questions, Goodman provides a list of "symp-toms of the aesthetic" that include "repleteness."[9] He uses the term *replete* to mark out distinctive criteria for works of art, without implying that they are good or bad art, but distinguishing them from maps, charts, and diagrams.[10] It relates to internal cross-referencing. Clearly, a ring composition has a facility for repleteness.

A poem or painting is replete when all the elements fit and contribute to the whole design. It is "fittingness" applied to the internal relation between the features of the art object. Do they support each other, or do they jostle, jar, and intrude? The same for literature: Do the elements of this story fit together? Has the argument wandered from the original idea?

The term *replete* has nothing to do with the content of the art object. In this context there is no such thing as repleteness in general, and no way of suggesting that the perfection of a work of art depends on some general completeness of its cross-referencing. We cannot call up universal values in order to say that the less the work is parochial or narrow the more it is replete. Nor can we say that unless the work of art is universal in its reference it cannot be said to be replete. Repleteness makes no call for the work to be humanitarian, or to respect the heritage of the past, or to be sensitive to the pains of childbirth or to dangers to the environment.[11] The term is technical. All that benevolent concern is dissipated when we focus on an original project and its fulfillment.

The book of Numbers provided an example of a ring with a defective ending (Chapter 5 above). Instead of pausing to recall the middle, the ending of the book goes straight home to the start. Neither of its two endings refers to the midpoint; the effect is disjointed in spite of elaborate care to make the other required cross-references.

The first and main ending makes an excellent connection with the beginning but somehow fails to connect up with the mid-turn. The failure is all the more noticeable in that the ending chapters are exemplary in ticking off, as it were, all the points made at the start when God commanded a census of the people of Israel (chs. 1–4). At the mid-turn the Levites had rebelled and been punished. When they turn up for mention in the first ending (ch. 35), instead of rebuke they receive forty-eight cities to live in, as if the chapter followed straight on from the exposition. There they have been told they cannot have a tribal territory, so some arrangement has to be made for them to have somewhere to live. Nothing is said about their revolt against Moses. Perhaps they have been forgiven, so perhaps no explanation is necessary, but there does seem to be a gap.

The second ending is the latch (ch. 36), where we would look in vain for some mention of the Levites. It follows on the first ending, but makes a quick switch of subject. The whole style of this book is almost everywhere rigidly consistent with ring practice. It uses, with textbook correctness, alternation and chiastic forms for indicating structural units. The exposition has placed the Levites in a servile position in the Temple, the mid-turn passionately records the Levites' perfidy. After such meticulous allegiance to the conventions, we expect the endings to follow the time-worn principles. We are entitled to expect some criticism of the Levites in the ending, but there is nothing. Clearly the editors were fully capable, and probably willing, so I assume the plan laid down in the exposition was interrupted. The text we have before us in chapter 35 has lost some and gained some additional material that forms the latch.[12]

Is it due to inadvertence? Why would the careful editors grow tired? Anyway, there is no other sign that they were tired. In the census of twelve tribes the exposition has given three places for the Josephites they are wishing to protect: one for Benjamin and one for each of the two sons of Joseph (three heirs, instead of the one heir each given to the other patriarchs in these lists). The Josephites' claim to be counted with the children of Israel has no other precedent in the book. We are not ever told that anyone has challenged it. We are not told why they need high-level support from the mouth of Moses himself. This latch is discomfiting. If it does confer extra cohesion, it applies at an unarticulated level of political loyalties. So correct in every other way, at the end the book of Numbers turns out to be a flawed ring.

We have seen the perfect exemplar, the *Iliad*, whose middle and ending both depend directly on the beginning. If we want modern examples written without an expressly recognized tradition, we can easily find authors who deliberately intend to take their work along the homeward route. Laurence Sterne, just after the middle of *Tristram Shandy*, lets fall that he knows he is supposed to go back to the beginning: "all which being considered, and that you see 'tis morally impracticable for me to wind this round to where I set out" (6.33).

His carefully structured book justifies my enterprise by being modern, being greatly appreciated, being famous for lack of structure, and yet by his admitting that he expects to go back to his beginning, and doing so by a series of inversely ordered parallelisms.

Ring composition belonged to the high style, an elegant form of writing for reciting at important events. As such it called for a proper ending. For other elegant literary forms, even more constrained by stylistic demands, such as pattern poems, endings were achieved in different ways.[13] For example, a text could be projected on a physical model. A pattern poem cuts the lines of a poem shorter and longer so as to depict on the page a figure of the subject of the work: the lines on the page present an outline, the poem and the image converge. This convention gives no scope for varied endings. When the lines of poetry have completed the visual shape on the page, the poet must stop or the picture will be spoiled. There is no need to herald an ending, no decision to be taken; the ending was implicated in the initial design.

The fashion in Europe for figure or pattern poems, starting from the Hellenistic tradition, was strong in the Middle Ages and even more popular in the late Renaissance. "Virtually every seventeenth-century poet attempted one or two. The design on the printed page is a pattern of the theme. Poets seem to have taken a special pleasure in the visual aesthetics of print."[14] Sometimes it seems to have been a kind of charming, clever decoration, more like a game or a greeting card. Alastair Fowler also shows that the pattern poem could be more than a gimmick; the poet found contemplative depth in reflecting on the analogy between the visual and verbal presentation (Fig. 15).[15]

In modeling the structure of a book upon the structure of a physical object, the book of Leviticus goes several steps further. This book is a projection of the tabernacle. God dictated the proportions of the

Alcimedontis
Poculum;
Illuſtrib. illuſtriß. & celſiß. Pr.
ac D. D. MAVRITII, *Haßiæ Landgravii; &c.*
Et generoſiß. inclutaḉ virg. D. AGNETÆ, *Comitiſſa à Solms; &c.*
noverum conjugum nuptiis; in aula Caſſellana magnifico & regio adparatu
IX. Kal. IIXbr. Anno ∞I⊃xcIII. *ſolemniter celebratis: in* Epithalamio; *cujus*
ἐπιγραφή: ECLOGA NUPTIALIS: *ſub perſona* Sylvani; *humilimæ congratu-*
LATIONIS & BONI OMINIS ERGO PROPINATVM, A
BERNH. PRÆTORIO, JESPVRG. P. L.

MAGNIFICAS ALII GAZA S DONANT: QVID EGO? VA H!
ARTE LUDI, ET TRUNCO T ORNATA TOREUMATA CESTR O.
Vanum opus ergò agitans, Ludensḉ; omnes operas heî C,
R em ta-men i-ſtam au-ſi M; faveât mihi numina tantù M!
Interea, dum aurum ſpl Endens, & pri Ma metall A,
C ādētesḉ feru N t gēmas, Numero abſḉ; Ego, ne ni L
Ipſe ſerà, hu N c cyathū, Sectum de ju Nipero, ecc E,
O ffero; pr ogeniem qv I Cattæ genti ſadumbra T
H aut facili Modulo, ne C cuiḉ ſat ben B a-pert O:
A djūcta & D omus eſt S Olmētis, & ip ſius ace R
Stirps, ḉ per longum ja Mēpus non-l Evenome N
Suſtinet; e- r i- miæ v- Ir-tutis laude r ro-bat A.
O bñ cône r i! ô qvæſa T vos di-vi- re laude T
Rhythmo vo r̃? verſu qv Is ſat gra-t ᵹur opim O
V ates? vi r Naſo præſt A ret maxi meus iſthu C.
M acti eſte, illuſtres; a-Gite; hec ego P ᵹibo pocl A
R epleta(ace ſpite, ô pro Ni, non æg ᵹiùs ac me L
E lyſium) innumerâ ſ Egete, ambroſ iaḉ perēn I,
Germina multa thori veſ Tri dent gaudia; qvæ ne C,
Im-pro-ba vis ra-pi-d Æſortis conturbet, iniqv E
C on-cita; nec ſe-clo Contra qvid ſe erigat ull O!
E ſſe velint etiam t Halami pia numina ple M
L ongævam, ſupe R et cuî diu ſple N:
Suo patr I qvæ ſit pb E
In omnibu Spar, & ſua M
S ub riſu ame T matrem viden S!
S it felix adeò, ſit ſ Orte beatus in omn I
Illuſtris patriæ noſtrę D ux, inclutaḉve eju S
M ens, ſimilem c v I nul-la vidi T
Ora: ore Cui lacte O,
Et brachiis E bur-ne-i S
T e-net nul-la, Nec obtinebit ull A
A dſimilem: hoc par h V ic eſt ſuper orbe nihi L.
L udite, dum licitum eſt, p rimævi veris in ort V,
Magnanimûm ſangven pa T rum; vos dextra guberne T
A lma Dei; in Pylium re, pr I nceps MAURICI, ad uſqv E,
Et te in Cumæum, ſpon S a incluta, ſoſpitet ævu M.

Fig. 15. The Goblet, from Bernhard Praetorius, "Alcimendontis Poculum",
Press mark: HAB 49 Poet (3). Courtesy Herzog August Bibliothek
Wolfenbüttel: 49 Poet. (8).

desert tabernacle to Moses in the book of Exodus (ch. 25). The build-ing consists of three compartments separated by two screens: the first, very large, the entrance and the court where the worshippers make sacrifice; the next, smaller, the sanctuary where only the priests may enter. It contains the table for the showbread, the altar of incense, and the *menorah*, the seven-branched candelabra. Lastly, the smallest, the Holy of Holies, contains the Mercy seat and the Ark of the Covenant, a figure of a cherubim on each side. Nobody can enter it except the high priest.

The book is likewise organized in three sections of diminishing size. It consists of laws, separated by two narratives, which I take to correspond to the two screens. The sections of the book preserve the relative proportions of the sections of the tabernacle. The first large section of the book corresponds to the large court of sacrifice, and the book's contents in this section actually state the laws for sacrifice. The second section of the book is smaller; it ordains the liturgical work of the priests through the year and prescribes rules for their marriages and households. In this respect it corresponds faithfully to the holy place reserved for priests, and it describes what has to be done with the incense, oil, and bread whose furnishings are in that compart-ment. The third part of the book is very small indeed, like the Holy of Holies, only three chapters long: it is about the covenant that is supposed to be kept there. So the book has been carefully projected upon the architecture of the tabernacle and on the proper activities of the place.

When the book comes to the pages that correspond to the end of the building it is modeled upon, it has automatically come to an end. To go on would spoil the design.[16] The analogy between the abstract structure of the written contents and the solid object on whose shape it has been projected gives the book a strange trans-parency. The reader looks through the words, or past them, and, visualizing the object, can intuit the depths of the analogy. At first Leviticus looked like a dry list of laws, but now, seeing it in three dimensions, it exemplifies the House of God. That does change the way it is read. And moreover, the tabernacle where God dwells among his people exemplifies Mount Sinai, where God originally met his people and gave his laws to Moses. Tabernacle, holy book, and holy mountain, presented so compactly, yet so vast in reference, mirroring each other in two and three dimensions, they stand for everything that is covered by God's law.

The pattern poem is a way for a text to say more than it says. This solves a theological difficulty. Frank Kermode, on the idea of the classic, reflects on "the difficulties we encounter when we ask what happens when modern minds engage ancient texts. From day to day we must cope with the paradox that the classic changes, yet retains its identity. It would not be read, and so would not be a classic, if we could not in some way believe it to be capable of saying more than its author meant; even, if necessary, that to say more than he meant was what he meant to do."[17]

The poem is undeniably a way of saying more than the words say, and even of saying more than the author could possibly have meant. In the case of Leviticus the hidden analogy has expanded the meaning to encompass the Lord's ordering of his infinite universe.

Seeing the Leviticus text as a projection of the tabernacle is a revelation of the same order as produced by reading a ring according to its structure. The impact of a composition would obviously be much enriched by having a meta-structure. If the verbal structure is being projected on to something else outside itself, it is making another analogy at a meta-poetic level. And this projection provides a further kind of ending or completion.

The previous pages have shown that the task of coming back to the starting point (the defining feature of ring composition) accounts for its complexities and its frailty. Asking why the author burdens the task of writing with the problems of return, we can suggest that writers and readers share a home-seeking urge. The effect of the ending on the overall coherence of a ring composition is crucial. If the ending does not perform all its functions, neatly connecting up the various themes that have gone before and picking out the key points like a street lamp, readers are excused for losing their way.

There is nothing final about homecoming. Any recognized kind of ending is loaded with intimations of other endings. After a rest, the home-comer will set out again, and return again. Nonetheless, with the sight of the place and the familiar smells and sounds, everything announces "home." No matter how many more expeditions there will be, each successive return to the start is an ending. A series of minor endings is characteristic of large works, like chapters in a book. By analogy, there is no reason to expect that each literary ending is final; an ending says only that some part of the work in hand is complete. More volumes may follow, like the four of the Pentateuch that follow Genesis. Their sequencing may have been anticipated, as in an alphabetic ordering.

Endings are not all happy; there are the griefs of failure, defeat, and death. The analogies press upon each other. No wonder that many agents who are free to choose, like writers and painters, will try to postpone ending. Whether they succeed depends on how much autonomy they enjoy. Social convention has to put out a heavy hand to oblige artists and players to stop.

The idea of reciprocity that governs all kinds of transactions underpins an idea of ending. An unrequited debt is waiting to be settled; requital makes an ending. Justice and fairness, punishment and revenge, and the great series of tit-for-tat exchanges, they all depend on construction of substitutability, they expect correct requital, neither too much nor too little, and at a stipulated time. At micro-levels the measuring of equivalence for matching gift and counter-gift may be free, but for important transactions the community eventually comes to help its members by imposing agreed techniques for calculating requital.

Time limits for settlement may be significant, if coordination is important. Gate money and box-office institutions require time limits. Some games need both a whistle to signal the beginning and a fixed time for play. Some firmly fix the ending into the structure of the game, as in some card games: when all the cards have been drawn, or when the players have all had their turn, the game must stop.

Without some external pressure, most writers have difficulty in knowing when to stop revising. Painters and sculptors are reluctant to lay down whatever they are using, knife, brush, or chisel. Sometimes the inspiration for the next work may push the current one into the background of concern, and so it ends at the point at which the artist is bored. Competition between artists can make it harder for one to relinquish the work if there is still a chance to do better than the rivals. Musical composers, painters, writers may only stop when they feel like it if they have the sole responsibility for structuring their own piece. As soon as their work involves collaboration, however, as a composer with an orchestra, a journalist with a newspaper, a painter with gallery officials, the need for coordination makes endings a matter of negotiation and convention. It means that the kind of pressure on ending according to conventions results from the kind of society that is giving out the rulings.

Social motives (like competition) may tempt an artist to postpone the ending for a long time. J. M. W. Turner used to send his pictures in to the Academy in a very rough state, expecting to finish them in the three days allowed for "varnishing." He was not the only painter to go on finishing his picture while it was hanging on the wall of the exhibition, but he made a big performance of it. Lawrence Gowing wrote of Turner: "One of the motives of the performances on the varnishing days was certainly to demonstrate the force that the intrinsic color of painting possessed in his hands, overwhelming every other artist. They were the final manifestations of power to out-rival everyone, past and present. His contemporaries retaliated; soon the galleries were full of painters tuning up their pictures in competition and the rooms reverberated with color."[18]

Different literary kinds require different kinds of endings. Obviously, any old conclusion cannot be foisted on any composition. It has to have been anticipated to some extent by the process of construction. The result of a mathematical accounting process can be indubitably correct; there is no room for interpretation. For a work of fiction interpretation is free. Its ending may have been prepared by building up some sort of crescendo, or by some steady decline heralding dissolution. Or, if neither of these is appropriate, the acceptable ending may review what has gone before. Fashion always exerts a constraining grip; there is always less autonomy and scarcer option for eccentric endings than we imagine.

These thoughts suggest further that "homing" is another of our fundamental mental resources, like making analogies and parallelisms. It is worth reflecting more on the gratification of going home, and the balance between the joy of exploring and the joy of returning. The traveler sets out with a destination in mind, reaches it, turns around, and travels back the same route to the beginning. Even very small animals, or insects, can do it. A mouse sallies forth from its retreat to get food, gets some, then turns around, comes back the same way, and arrives. Through our animal origins we are gifted with navigational skills, which we recognize when we watch a homing pigeon or track wasps to their nest.[19] Some deep-laid faculty has nurtured this process in human beings. We know what homing means; we do it all the time, we can recognize a return to the beginning when we see it, and we can transpose it to a literary form. It would be satisfying for this argument if we were able to say that,

> . . . the end of all our exploring
> Will be to arrive where we started
> And know the place for the first time.
> Through the unknown, remembered gate
> When the last of earth left to discover
> Is that which was the beginning. (T. S. Eliot, *Little Gidding*, V)[20]

No wonder the ending is so important for a long ring composition: it can link together everything in the text, creating coherence for the whole. When the ending of a composition wraps up everything that is there, the whole is endowed with a special power. The same for a painting or a carving, or music — its dense coherence inspires feelings of respect, even of awe. It is something to be valued for itself, like poetry, regardless of what narrative or instrumental functions it may perform. You might use the picture for a blanket, the carving to stop a leak, the poem to advertise a brand drink.[21] Its possible usefulness is irrelevant to its quality as a work of art. The thing is too impressive to be cherished for generations because of any incidental ability it may have to refer to something outside itself. It is not made for a practical purpose, like a map. It is not necessarily made for a limited occasion, such as a graveside elegy, a marriage blessing, a speech for a school prize-giving. It is made to be itself, a complete thing in its own right. This explains why the ring has a formal ending, but it does not say why it has died out in so many places. Nor does it solve Jakobson's conundrum. Another chapter on endings will be necessary to do justice to both thoughts.

After all this, Jakobson's paradox is unchanged. We believe what he says, that writing in parallels comes to everyone naturally — but we do not understand why we are slow to recognize it. Recall that I wish to understand both why ring composition fell out of fashion in the east Mediterranean hinterland in the fourth and fifth centuries, and also why now we have trouble recognizing rings.

I suspect that I have not been explicit enough about this latter difficulty. Let me take advantage of the latch to give at the very end one more case of a typical misreading of a ring. Erich Auerbach's interpretation of Bishop Gregory's *Histories of the Franks* illustrates how easy it is to mistake the genre and the motives of the writer if the central loading is not recognized.[1] Saint Gregory was the Bishop of Tours in the sixth century, and he was highly esteemed in his time. Auerbach saw a big contrast between the bishop's degenerate, decadent form of writing and the classical Latin of the previous period when Roman splendor was at its height. He recognized Gregory as a famous, influential writer in his period; he praised his style as vivid, psychologically superb, dramatic, and emotional. But he deplored its being repetitive and over-detailed. He especially drew attention to the syntactical control by which the Roman prose of the Golden Age made connections that "reach the height of subtlety, exactness and diversity — an observation which applies not only to conjunctions and other devices of subordination, but also to the use of tenses, word order, antithesis and numerous other rhetorical devices, which are likewise made to serve the same end of exact, subtle, yet pliable and richly shaded disposition. . . . Gregory's language, on the other hand, is but imperfectly equipped to organize facts; as soon as a complex of events ceases to be very simple, he is no longer able to present it as a coherent whole. His language organizes badly, or not at all."[2]

The point that concerns me here is the charge that Gregory is just not able to present his story coherently, implying intellectual weakness. Auerbach compares Gregory's style in which, for lack of a controlling syntax, words and emotions come gushing out, with classical Latin, where "the whole is strictly controlled by the order imposed by impersonal syntax, the sense is infinitely richer and better articulated." Though he praises Gregory's style for its immediacy and sensory directness, he finds that the text gives an "impression of disorder," it is "confused and imprecise," there is "a general lack of orderly arrangement in the grammatical structure." He concludes "that Gregory is not capable of arranging the occurrences themselves in an orderly fashion."[3] Auerbach pours scorn on the boorish, country-bumpkin style. He may praise it for being concrete, sensory, spontaneous, but he dismisses it as utterly disorganized and weak in syntax.

This ought to present Auerbach with a puzzle, since he fully recognizes that the good breeding and education of the bishop implied that he would have been capable of writing in the classical style. He also notes that Gregory himself had said emphatically that he knew his style seemed boorish, but that he had deliberately adopted it so that his *Histories of the Franks* would be more accessible to his congregation. The story Auerbach has selected to exemplify Gregory's writing turns out to be a ring composition, which imposes its own syntactical rules and frame of reference. Gregory believed that this style would be more widely understood than the rigid grammatical formulae of the classical Latin writers. Choosing to write like this was for him what Martin Heinzelmann calls "pastoral strategy."[4]

The story is about a blood feud between two men. By the end of the story the words and actions of the beginning are repeated in inverse order. In the first scene, a servant is struck with a sword and falls down dead. Sicharius, the central character, tries to avenge him; fighting ensues, the would-be avenger (Sicharius) escapes. In the last scene it is Sicharius who is struck with a sword and falls down dead, and the servant who escapes. Auerbach gibes at the word-for-word repetition. He does not notice that the first statement, about being struck with a sword and falling down dead, and its inverted form at the end, make the *inclusio* for the whole story.

As it is a tit-for-tat tale of revenge told in clear parallelisms we should look for the middle to see what it is all about. The central place is not difficult to find. The story comprises three episodes, each about a crime and the court's verdict on it. The middle crime with the court that tried it is at the central place between the other two; all three are presented as parallelisms. The three episodes trace the development of the feud, with violations of the peace on an escalating scale, the crimes more horrendous each time. In each episode the status of the court also escalates, so first, the people's court, second, the judges' and the bishop's court, and last, in highest degree of judicial rank, the city court.

The first two courts require *wergild* to be paid, but compensation is refused each time by the offended party, who intends to wreak his own revenge. The third trial results in a reconciliation of the two enemy avengers. But after all that carnage, justice was not seen to have been done, the two avengers have both gotten off lightly. The last big scandal is that both refused to accept compensation; both persisted in murderous vengeance till the end. But the story goes on. The two enemies make friends, then they quarrel, and one, suddenly enraged by a tasteless joke, does kill his friend in a final revenge. This is the last scene, which repeats the first in reverse: Sicharius is killed and the servant escapes.

Auerbach was misled by the title of the book; the stories were not meant for a history for historians. The bishop's court is central. The whole object and meaning of the story is there. Bishop Gregory's long sermon on Christian peace and his fervent denunciation of feud and vengeance are in the middle. We must conclude that the text is a message for the faithful about the teaching of the Church. That is why Gregory has used the simple language of everyday and dispensed with the strict and rigid grammatical structures of the high style — precisely as he had said. The little puzzle about why someone so well educated as Gregory should compose in such a simple manner disappears.

Auerbach's reproaches against inelegant Latin and "grammatical monsters" do not concern us so much as his claim that Gregory's text is unintelligible and his thinking muddled. He says that the history has left out what was necessary and included much unnecessary detail; the reader is left in the dark. Gregory lacks historical judgment: he has chosen to write about minor episodes, so trivial that no classical historian would have bothered to mention them at all. Auerbach evidently considers not only the syntax to be weak but the author to be weak in the head.

Qualified scholars have turned the edge of his censure against the critic, in defense of Gregory.[5] Auerbach's scoffing remarks about Gregory's inability to see his work as a whole and his sneers about incoherence, disorder, and mental confusion are misguided. You cannot mistake the bishop's sermon on Christian teaching for the meanderings of a feeble-minded historian *manqué*, not when you know how the framework has been constructed and you know what is in the middle.

At this point, we should try to take stock of ourselves and our own cultural environment. Gregory's histories lost out in comparison with classical Latin writings, which belonged to such a different civilization. It is possible that now that ring compositions have started to reemerge from a long period of neglect they also find themselves in the wrong kind of civilization.

Part of the answer to why ring composition has died out will be that nowadays its very repleteness has a downside. To some it may seem too highly contrived. Take away one word, change the pronunciation of another, the fittingness is compromised. It becomes difficult to know what was meant. It calls for a high degree of connoisseurship in the composers and readers, but connoisseurs easily disappear. Without their steady social support the balanced cross-references and delicate symmetries will be a liability. The more replete it is, the more precarious the constituent correspondences will be in their reliance on each other. According to discussions of postmodernism, we are now living in a culture that resists boundaries and shuns formal endings. In literature, painting, and music, there is a preference for openness, part of a more general bias against formality and structure. If that is true, it may account for some of the current difficulties in reading these firmly bounded, well-structured writings.

If we are indeed in a period that prefers open-ended solutions, then we ourselves might risk going a step further in open-endedness. We could try questioning the popular idea that postmodernism is a unique state, experienced only by the generations that have reacted against the certainties and confidence of the Renaissance. If we are in such a period we can also be open to the thought that we are not unique, and that the explanation for the disappearance of ring composition in various regions was the result each time of recurring states of mind very similar to our own. We can try the idea that postmodern uncertainty and skepticism are examples of a cultural undercurrent that surfaces when the pillars of a local modernism are shaken and the old system is coming to grief.

When an antique piece of furniture, ornament, or style of painting that has once been valued, then has been disvalued, and then resuscitated in general esteem, Rubbish Theory applies.[6] The expiry or survival of objects does not depend on any natural robustness. Old lace and old ceramics in themselves are very perishable. Like everything else once valued, they could eventually fall out of fashion and be chucked on the midden. A change of fashion may change their status into delicate antiques, but it only works to save a few of the relegated objects. A vast majority are destroyed as rubbish. Things can endure only if they are so highly valued that resources are dedicated to their preservation. The natural perishability of these ancient relics accounts for why only a few examples remain.

A literary genre that survives through many centuries, even millennia, is not a specially tough or resilient medium; it survives because it has been seen to be worth protecting. Its survival is like the survival of old lace, wrapped in protective tissues and cherished by its owners (or museum curators). The initial question was why the merits of ring composition are still disregarded even now that they are resurfacing after aeons of oblivion. Why is no one noticing the elegant correspondences and witty puns, or enjoying the titillating analogies that resonate across the structure? The same Rubbish Theory states that once an object has become classified as rubbish it becomes invisible. No one notices it, no one even sees it. Only after many decades a few examples may be fished out of the darkness and slime, cleaned up, and placed in glass cases. Then they are formally transformed into durable objects and acknowledged as genuine antiques. Then anyone will at once perceive their value, and the archaeologists will start digging for more of them.

It follows that survival depends on contemporary esteem. Any genre is at risk from social change. Not only genres — de Saussure, the great philologist, was deeply pessimistic about discourses, or words, or even letters, retaining stable meanings over any short period, or even between performances. I mean pessimistic in the sense of extreme doubt, simple skepticism, not in any sense of sadness, rather in the excitement of an important discovery about truth.[7] Indeed, it is an important topic. It is hard for anyone raised in a modernist culture ever to imagine that the value of truth could be diminished. By "modernist" I mean one whose unchallenged categories make strong boundaries and which supports the categories with functioning institutions. Yet this diminishing is what many Bible scholars dread from the questioning of historical truths. David Damrosch puts his finger on the mood: "In this way, a desire for living truth may bring the canonical critic rather close to the hermeneutic relativism of poststructuralist and deconstructionist literary theorists, who apply a Nietzschean philosophy of language to argue for the radical indeterminacy of all meaning."[8]

A culture of uncertainty implies radical indeterminacy. Its prophet and spokesman was Jorge Luis Borges. Evelyn Fishburn quotes him: "If I am rich in anything, it is in perplexities, not in certainties" was Borges's upbeat way of expressing what Jean-François Lyotard would later call the postmodernist loss of faith in grand narratives. An essential skepticism permeates his work, seeking constantly to undermine our belief in all systems of knowledge and global explanations, and indeed questioning the very possibility for such systems to exist. Rather than in their truth, their value would lie, for Borges, in their ability to astonish, that is to say, as "branches of the literature of fantasy."[9]

It is difficult to write about the end of the fashion for composing in rings without recognizing a present fashion against closure in our own culture. In a brilliant chapter entitled "Closure and Anti-Closure in Modern Poetry," Barbara Herrnstein Smith says that our contemporary poets seem "to reflect a general preference for, and deliberate cultivation of the *expressive* qualities of weak closure: even when the poem is finally closed, it is not usually slammed shut — the lock may be secure, but the 'click' has been muffled." Alongside of this trend, she notes that the traditional forms of poetic ending are still used and respected. But in "all contemporary art anti-closure is a recognizable impulse," and it "reflects changing presumptions concerning the nature of art itself."[10]

In a culture of mistrust, language itself becomes suspect and deceiving. In the same book Smith says: "What is particularly significant for poetry, as opposed here to art and music, is the suspicion of language. . . . Language is the badge of our suspect reason and humanity. It is the lethal trap sprung for truth; it is the reliquary of the mortmain of the past; it categorizes and codifies, obliterating the complexities, subtleties and ambiguities of experience."[11] She goes on to say: "Postmodernism is not simply concerned with dismantling the Enlightenment's notion of an ascertainable, objective truth, or with distinguishing between truths and falsehood. . . . But with proposing the notion of a decentered reality in which a multiplicity of truths collide in an unhierarchical existence."[12]

Total mistrust and a change of reality — this is powerful stuff, way beyond my sights. Yet it illumines my central question. We, living in the postmodernist age, are "perhaps the heir to too many revolutions . . . we know too much and are sceptical of all that we know, feel and say. All traditions are equally viable because all are equally suspect. Where conviction is seen as self-delusion and as all last words are lies, the only resolution may be in the affirmation of irresolution, and conclusiveness may be soon seen as not only less honest but *less stable* than inconclusiveness."[13] Too much change and too much challenge to belief, these could be the times in which a polished ring composition would not be the right medium for expressing what is uppermost in readers' minds.

If a culture is indeed heavily against boundaries, rules, and closures as such, the ring shape would seem too formal, artificial, mechanical. It will not be popular when the preference is for natural spontaneity. Instead of being taken for granted as a normal thing, the very idea of closure is felt to be ambiguous. Is it not better to remain open? Smith describes a postmodern tendency toward anti-closure in all the arts and humanities.[14] It is true. Our own is an example of a culture averse to artistic and poetic closure. Modern painting should not have a finished look, modern music avoids closure, postmodern literature exemplifies the trend by keeping suspense alive, leaving all possibilities open.

We tend to assume that postmodernism is something that has only happened to ourselves. It cannot be invoked to explain changes of bias in ancient civilizations. What we learn about postmodern aversion to sharp endings would seem irrelevant to the venerable cultures that first wrote and then allowed ring compositions to lapse. Some readers will protest that postmodernism is a unique manifestation of our Western history. But without having been through the Enlightenment, plausible symptoms of the same syndrome can be found in other periods and places.

Civilizations may rest on different principles of organization. Resorting to cultural theory, I will need to distinguish competitive individualism from hierarchy.[15] The first culture is opportunistic; it pushes for change and has to find ways of dealing with problems of identity and uncertainty without blocking innovation. It is attuned to change; its view of past and future is short term. The other culture is traditionalist: it tries to put a brake on competition, it reveres and memorializes the past, and it has a long-term perspective.[16]

Even ancient societies go through traditionalist and opportunistic phases. For an example of change from one to another, I cite Katrina McLeod's fine essay "The Political Culture of Warring States China."[17] From the eighth to the seventh centuries BCE the Chinese Chou dynasty was defeated by the Western barbarians. Formerly the Chou kings were "redistributive chiefs." They had been at the center of a feudal-style network of giving and receiving; in return for land, families, horses, chariots, and precious metals given to sub-chiefs, they took tribute and military service. After they were de-feated, the new kind of regime was based on individual negotiation; political leadership and military organization developed competi-tively. The various states achieved varying degrees of centralization. They competed with each other, made covenants to regulate their affairs, continually broke their alliances, until a few large states even-tually emerged. Large numbers of skilled, literate, younger members of the competing lineages who found themselves without any ter-ritorial allegiance or institutional constraints, became expert in new technologies of weaponry, strategy, metallurgy, and fortification and had much to offer to the new class of peripatetic generals and man-agers of the estates. By the fifth to the third centuries, the period of the Warring States, Chinese culture had become thoroughly individ-ualistic, entrepreneurial, and competitive. Strikingly relevant to the theme of closure, certainty had disappeared, and so had cognitive coherence and confidence in language.

The perception of cognitive dissonance in the philosophical texts was underlined by what Arthur Waley has called the "language crisis" of the period. "Warring States philosophers wrote about their per-ception that words (literally 'names') and objects (literally the 'solid' or 'really existing') no longer matched or corresponded."[18]

The ancient Chinese concern for cognitive coherence and lan-guage suggestively echoes the contemporary concerns with language and uncertainty. We ourselves with wars and changing technology have been shifting into a more opportunistic mood, and in certain aesthetic fields we have a bias against hard-and-fast lines, boundaries, and endings. Such political shifts, entailing similar effects, could hap-pen anywhere at any time. After the debilitating wars with Persia, could a Greek precursor of this modern aesthetic mood have caused ring composition to fall out of fashion? If so, it may explain some of our scholarly tendency to rubbish it.

Rules for endings and beginnings are only symptoms. The whole structure of the ring is rule bound, this without constraining the creative energies of the poet. After a major revolution or after a prolonged war, the survivors long for new forms of expression and signal their own vitality by rejecting the old. I will take license to answer Jakobson's conundrum by reference to social and cultural causes. The same factors that cause ring composition to lose repute in the first place could have been at work with us over the past fifty years to hide it from our vision.

NOTES

Chapter 1. Ancient Rings Worldwide

1. Glenn W. Most, *The Measures of Praise: Structure and Function in Pindar's Second Pythian and Seventh Nemean Odes* (Gottingen: Vandenhoeck and Ruprecht, 1985), 11.
2. Jack R. Lundbom, "The Inclusio and Other Framing Devices in Deuteronomy 1–28," *Vetus Testamentum* 46 (1966): 296–315.
3. Jacob Milgrom, *Numbers: The Traditional Hebrew Text with the New JPS Translation* (Philadelphia: Jewish Publication Society, 1990).
4. Robert Lowth, *De Sacra Poesi Hebraeorum.* The Oxford Lectures on Poetry (1753; trans. Boston, 1829), 157ff.
5. Milgrom, *Numbers*, xxii.
6. Roman Jakobson and Krystyna Pomorska, *Dialogues*, trans. Christian Hubert (Cambridge: Cambridge University Press, 1983), 102.
7. James Fox, "Roman Jakobson and the Comparative Study of Parallelism," in *Roman Jakobson: Echoes of His Scholarship*, ed. C. H. van Schooneveld and D. Armstrong (Lisse: De Ritter Press, 1977).
8. Jakobson and Pomorska, *Dialogues*, 103.
9. Quoted in ibid., 102.
10. Quoted in ibid.
11. Martin Schwartz, "The Gathas and Other Old Avestan Poetry," in *La Langue Poétique Indo-européenne*, ed. G.-J. Pinault and D. Petit (Paris, 2006), 1.
12. H.-P. Schmidt, "Die Komposition von Yasna 49," in *Prati Danum, F. J. Kuiper (London: Mouton, 1968)*, 170–92. Martin Schwartz, "Gathic Compositional History, Y29 and Bovine Symbolism," in *Paitimana: Essays in Iranian, Indo-European, and Indian Studies in Honor of Hanns-Peter Schmidt*, vol. 2, ed. Siamak Adhami (Costa Mesa: Mazda, 2006), 194–249.
13. Schwartz, "Gathic Compositional History," 196.
14. Léon Vandermeersch, "Les origines divinatoires de la tradition chinoise du paraléllisme littéraire," *Extrême-Orient-Extrême-Occident* 11 (1989): 11–32.
15. Sarah Allan, *The Shape of the Turtle: Myth, Art, and Cosmos in Early China* (Albany: SUNY Press, 1981).

16. I am grateful to the Czech sinologist Milena Dolezelova for opening to me this aspect of the history of parallelism.

17. Vandermeersh, "Les origines divinatoires."

18. Ibid.

19. Hua L. Wu, "The Concept of Parallelism: Jin Shengtan's Critical Discourse on *The Water Margins*," in *Poetics East and West*, ed. Milena Dolezelova-Velingerova. Monograph Series of Toronto Semiotics 4 (Toronto, 1988–89), 170.

20. Milena Dolezelova-Velingerova, "Seventeenth-Century Chinese Theory of Narrative: A Reconstruction of Its System and Concepts," in *Poetics East and West*, 149–55.

21. Dolezelova-Velingerova, "Seventeenth-Century Chinese Theory of Narrative," quote on p. 152.

22. Robert Alter and Frank Kermode, *The Literary Guide to the Bible* (Cambridge, Mass.: Harvard University Press, 1987).

23. Robert Alter, "The Characteristics of Ancient Hebrew Poetry," in Alter and Kermode, *Literary Guide to the Bible*, 611–24; Joel Rosenberg, "Jeremiah and Ezekiel," in Alter and Kermode, *Literary Guide to the Bible*, 184–206.

24. Ibid., 190.

25. Simon Weightman, "Structure and the *Mathnawi*." Presented at the Rumi Conference, January 25–26, 2002, School of Oriental and African Studies (SOAS), and Islamic Centre of England. All quotes from Weightman from these papers.

26. Seyed Ghahreman Savi-Homani, " 'Love the Whole and Not the Part': Investigation of the Rhetorical Structure of Book One of the Mathnawī of Jalāl al-din Rumi" (D.Phil. thesis, University of London, 2003).

27. I am grateful to Eberhard Fincke for this information.

28. Albert Lord, *The Singer of Tales* (Cambridge, Mass.: Harvard University Press, 1960). For G. Nagy on creative recall, see his *Poetry as Performance* (Cambridge: Cambridge University Press, 1996), 16.

29. Jack Goody, *The Power of the Written Tradition* (Washington, D.C.: Smithsonian Institution Press, 2000), 21–22.

30. Aldous Huxley, *Vulgarity in Literature: Digressions from a Theme* (London: Chatto and Windus, 1930), 15.

31. Jean Starobinski, *Les Mots sous les Mots: Les anagrammes de Ferdinand Saussure* (Paris: Gallimard, 1971).

32. Douglas R. Hofstadter, *Le Ton Beau de Marot: In Praise of the Music of Language* (New York: Basic Books, 1997), 305.

33. Umberto Cassuto, *From Noah to Abraham* (Jerusalem: Magnes Press, 1997).
34. I thank Robert Murray for allowing me to publish this analysis of Genesis 2–3 from his unpublished lecture notes.

Chapter 2. Modes and Genres

1. Alastair Fowler, *Kinds of Literature: An Introduction to the Theory of Genres and Modes* (Cambridge, Mass: Harvard University Press, 1982), 18.
2. From Leonard B. Meyer's *Music, the Arts, and Ideas: Patterns and Predictions in Twentieth-Century Culture* (Chicago: University of Chicago Press, 1967), as quoted in Frank Kermode, *The Genesis of Secrecy: On the Interpretation of Narrative* (Cambridge, Mass.: Harvard University Press, 1979).
3. Ibid., 162.
4. W. A. van Otterlo, *De Ringcompositie als opbouwprincipe in de Epische Gedichten van Homerus* (Amsterdam: Verhandling der Koninklijke Nederlandsche Academie van Wetenschappen, 1948). Although the book is written in Dutch, Otterlo has appended a brief resumé in French.
5. G. B. Gray, *The Forms of Hebrew Poetry* (London and New York: Hodder and Stoughton, 1915), 37. (The *Iliad* is actually written in dactylic hexameters, so combining ring form and meter.)
6. This structure would correspond to that of the book of Numbers (which I shall show in Chapter 4) where the external ring narrates chronologically the epic journey of the people of Israel from Egypt to the Jordan and is systematically interrupted by catalogues of laws given by God to Moses and Aaron. (I am not sure, however, that the interruptions are in ring form.)
7. Jonathan Magonet, *Bible Lives* (London: SCM Press, 1991), 27.
8. I thank Sybil Stokes for going to look at the monument to check these details.
9. E. Auerbach, *Mimesis: The Representation of Reality in Western Literature* (Princeton, N.J.: Princeton University Press, 1953), 11.
10. Shalom Spiegel, *The Last Trial: On the Legends and Lore of the Command to Abraham to Offer Isaac as a Sacrifice: The Akedah* (New York: Behrman House, 1979), 110–11.
11. Sebastian Brock, "From Ephrem to Romanos," in *Greek Literature in the Byzantine Period: Greek Literature*, vol. 9, ed. Gregory Nagy (New York: Routledge, 2001), 1–151.
12. Isaac AQEDA, version from Romanos, listed in *Le Muséon* 99 (1986): 66–67.

13. Auerbach, *Mimesis*, ch. 1, "Odysseus' Scar."
14. This is my own interpretation of the famous passage that has received much attention. I have examined only eighteen verses of chapter 22. Rabbi Jonathan Magonet has published an analysis of the whole Abraham story, starting from God's call to Abraham in Genesis 12 and concluding at the end of chapter 22. Predictably, the mid-turn of this larger ring comes at a different place. Magonet, "Abraham," ch. 2 in *Bible Lives* (London: SCM Press, 1992), 23–33.
15. Vladimir Propp, *Theory and History of Folklore*, trans. A. Y. Martin and R. P. Martin, ed. A. Lieberman (Manchester: Manchester University Press, 1954).
16. Maurice Bloch, ed., *Political Language and Oratory in Traditional Society* (New York: Academic Press, 1975).
17. Emile Durkheim, *The Elementary Forms of the Religious Life: A Study in Religious Sociology*, trans. Joseph Ward Swain (London: G. Allen and Unwin, 1915).
18. Joseph Henrich and Francis Gill-White, "The Evolution of Prestige," *Evolution and Human Behavior* 22 (2001): 165–96.
19. B. W. Andrzejewski and I. M. Lewis, *Somali Poetry: An Introduction* (Oxford: Clarendon Press, 1964), 42.

Chapter 3. How to Construct and Recognize a Ring

1. J. W. Welch and D. B. McKinlay, eds., *Chiasmus Bibliography* (Provo, Utah: Research Press, 1999).
2. Ibid., 168–69.
3. Roland Meynet, *L'Analyse rhétorique: Une nouvelle méthode pour comprendre la Bible* (Paris: Les Editions du Cerf, 1989): "Il faut sentir à quel point ce parti contrecarre les habitudes. Il fait plus: il parait contrarier l'impression immédiate que le texte biblique produit sur le lecteur de l'occident, qui le trouve souvent malcomposé, pas composé du tout, heurte," 9.
4. Nils W. Lund, *Chiasmus in the New Testament* (Chapel Hill: University of North Carolina Press, 1942).
5. Umberto Cassuto, *From Noah to Abraham* (Jerusalem: Magnes Press, 1964).
6. Jonathan Magonet, *Form and Meaning: Studies in Literary Techniques in the Book of Jonah*, 2nd ed. (Sheffield: Almond Press, 1983).
7. Gary Rendsburg, *The Redaction of Genesis* (Winona Lake, Ind.: Eisenbrauns, 1986).

8. John Bligh, *Galatians: A Discussion of St. Paul's Epistle* (London: St. Paul Publications, 1969), 37–40.

9. Leonard Muellner, *The Anger of Achilles: Menis in Greek Epic* (Ithaca, N.Y.: Cornell University Press, 1996).

10. Gregory Nagy, *Poetry as Performance: Homer and Beyond* (Cambridge: Cambridge University Press, 1996), 16.

11. Alastair Fowler, *Kinds of Literature: An Introduction to the Theory of Genres and Modes* (Cambridge, Mass.: Harvard University Press, 1982), 29.

12. Douglas Hofstadter, *Le Ton Beau de Marot: In Praise of the Music of Language* (New York: Basic Books, 1997). My own experience as a member of the Highgate Limerick Society goes to support this opinion.

13. Ibid., 272.

14. Ibid.

Chapter 4. Alternating Bands: Numbers

1. Glenn W. Most, *The Measures of Praise: Structure and Function in Pindar's Second Pythian and Seventh Nemean Odes* (Gottingen: Vandenhoeck and Ruprecht, 1985).

2. Mary Douglas, *In the Wilderness: The Doctrine of Defilement in the Book of Numbers* (Sheffield: Sheffield Academic Press, 1993).

3. See David Meijers, "The Structural Analysis of the Jewish Calendar and Its Political Implications," *Anthropos* 82 (1987): 604–10.

4. David Goodman, "Note on Identifying Beginnings and Endings," in Douglas, *In the Wilderness*, 123–26.

5. Ibid.

6. David Goodman's note on two words for "trumpets," ibid., 141–43.

7. Quoted in Douglas, *In the Wilderness*, 123.

8. Goodman, "Note on Identifying Beginnings and Endings," 124.

9. Ibid., 125.

10. The list of endings for law sections is given in ibid., 126.

Chapter 5. The Central Place: Numbers

1. Mary Douglas, "Responding to Ezra: The Priests and the Foreign Wives," *Biblical Interpretation* 10, no. 1 (2002): 1–23.

2. Graeme Auld, ed., "Judges 1–.25, in The Conquest under the Leadership of the House of Judah," in *Understanding Poets and Prophets: Essays in Honour of G. A. Anderson* (Sheffield: Sheffield Academic Press, 1993);

M. Weinfeld, "The Period of the Conquest and the Judges as Seen by the Earlier and the Later Sources," *Vetus Testamentum* 17 (1967): 93–111.

3. J. Blenkinsopp, "The Judaean Priesthood during the Neo-Babylonian and Achaemenid Periods: A Hypothetical Reconstruction," *Catholic Biblical Quarterly* 60, no. 1 (1998): 25–43. I thank Gary Rendsburgh for alerting me to references to the sons of Aaron in important political roles in Joshua 22.13, 30–32; 24.33; Judges 20.28.

4. Mary Douglas, *Jacob's Tears: The Priestly Project of Reconciliation* (Oxford: Oxford University Press, 2004).

5. Graeme Auld, "After Exodus and Before Numbers," in *The Book of Leviticus: Composition and Reception*, ed. Rolf Rendtorf and Robert Kugler (Leiden: Brill, 2003), 41–54.

Chapter 6. Modern, Not-Quite Rings

1. Roman Jakobson: "There is a system of steady correspondences in composition and order of elements on many different levels: syntactic constructions, grammatical forms and grammatical categories, lexical synonyms and total lexical identities, and finally combinations of sounds and prosodic schemes." Roman Jakobson and Krystyna Pomorska, *Dialogues*, trans. Christian Hubert (Cambridge: Cambridge University Press, 1983), 102–3.

2. Rodney Needham discusses the idea of "natural universals" and warns that they cannot be expected to have the same interpretation across cultures. Needham, *Circumstantial Deliveries* (Berkeley: University of California Press, 1981), 59.

3. Evelyn Fishburn touches on these possibilities in a chapter in "Traces of the Thousand and One Nights in Borges," *Variaciones Borges* 17 (2004): 143–57.

4. Agatha Christie, *Five Little Pigs* (New York: Dodd, Mead, 1942).

5. Agatha Christie, *The ABC Murders* (reprint, New York: Dodd, Mead, 1977; orig. William Collins, 1936).

6. Thomas Narcejac, *Une Machine à lire: Le roman policier* (Paris: Denoël/Gonthier, 1975).

7. Ibid., 87.

8. The text used in this and the following chapter is from Laurence Sterne, *The Life and Opinions of Tristram Shandy, Gentleman*, ed. Melvyn New and Joan New, with an introductory essay by Christopher Ricks (New York: Penguin, 2003).

9. William Freedman, *Laurence Sterne and the Origin of the Musical Novel* (Athens: University of Georgia Press, 1978), 146–47.

10. Ibid., 29.

11. Sterne, *Tristram Shandy*, Appendix, Glossary of Terms of Fortification, 668.

12. Freedman, *Laurence Sterne*, 29.

Chapter 7. Tristram Shandy: *Testing for Ring Shape*

Some parts of this chapter were presented at the Christian Literary Studies Group conference, Corpus Christi College, Oxford, November 2000, and published as "Shandean Mirrors, Puzzles of the Master Analogy," in *The Glass* 14 (Winter 2001/Spring 2002): 14–29.

1. Robert Lowth, *De Sacra Poesi Hebraeorum*, based on thirty-four lectures in Latin delivered at Oxford between 1741 and 1750.

2. Alastair Fowler, *Triumphal Forms: Structural Patterns in Elizabethan Poetry* (Cambridge: Cambridge University Press, 1970).

3. Parenthetical references to *Tristram Shandy* refer to volume and chapter number.

4. The main Treaty of Utrecht, involving all the European powers, was finally signed in 1713. It achieved a complete reorganization of Europe, the dissolution of the Austrian empire, and the freeing of trade.

5. Uncle Toby received his wound and was invalided home in July of 1695, so some time has elapsed before the events of this book take place.

6. A collection of Greek and Latin religious and philosophical writings was ascribed to Hermes Trismegistus (first to third centuries A.D.) A fusion of Stoic, Neo-Pythagorean, and Eastern religious elements, with much cosmological and astronomical teaching. (See *The Oxford Dictionary of the Christian Church* [Oxford: Oxford University Press, 2005], s.v. "Hermetic Books.")

7. According to Campbell Ross, Sterne read and admired all three. Erasmus's protests against critics who objected to his rude attacks on theologians in *L'Eloge de la folie* are very similar to Sterne's own apologia in *Tristram Shandy*.

8. A point reiterated in Ian Campbell Ross's biography, *Laurence Sterne: A Life* (Oxford: Oxford University Press, 2001).

9. Ibid.

10. Christopher Ricks, "The Irish Bull," chapter 4 in his *Beckett's Dying Words* (Oxford: Clarendon Press, 1990), 153–56.

Chapter 8. Two Central Places, Two Rings: The Iliad

The text used in these chapters is Richard Lattimore's translation, *The Iliad of Homer* (Chicago: Chicago University Press, 1951).

1. John L. Myres, *Homer and His Critics*, ed. Dorothea Grey (London: Routledge & Paul, 1958), 46–47.
2. Jack Goody, *The Myth of the Bagre* (Oxford: Clarendon Press, 1972), 186–87.
3. E. D. Lewis, "A Quest for the Source: The Ontogenesis of a Creation Myth of the Ata Tana Ai," chapter 9 in *To Speak in Pairs, Essays on the Ritual Languages of Eastern Indonesia*, ed. James J. Fox (Cambridge: Cambridge University Press, 1988).
4. Oliver Taplin, *Homeric Soundings: The Shaping of the Iliad* (Oxford: Clarendon Press, 1992).
5. Ibid., 15.
6. Cedric Whitman, *Homer and the Heroic Tradition* (Cambridge, Mass.: Harvard University Press, 1958), 257.
7. Ibid., 256.
8. Parenthetical references are to book and line number; thus, in this case, book 24, lines 665–67.
9. Whitman, *Homer and the Heroic Tradition*, 257.
10. Alastair Fowler, *Triumphal Forms: Structural Patterns in Elizabethan Poetry* (Cambridge: Cambridge University Press, 1970).

Chapter 9. Alternating Nights and Days: The Iliad

1. Arthur Hatto introduced this term to me, with many lively examples and the reference to the volume he edited called *Traditions of Heroic and Epic Poetry*, vol. 2 (London: Modern Humanities Research Association, 1989).
2. G. E. Duckworth, *Structural Patterns and Proportions in Virgil's Aeneid: A Study in Mathematical Composition* (Ann Arbor: University of Michigan Press, 1962).
3. Malcolm Willcock, *A Companion to the Iliad: Based on the Translation by Richmond Lattimore* (Chicago: Chicago University Press, 1976), 82, relating to 7.421: "This is still the same morning, Idaios' visit to the Greek camp has taken place very early. Line 433, this must be the dawn of a new day."

4. Cedric Whitman, *Homer and the Heroic Tradition* (Cambridge, Mass.: Harvard University Press, 1958), 257.

5. Ibid.

Chapter 10. The Ending: How to Complete a Ring

1. I acknowledge stimulus on the competitive aspects of a bard's recital from Douglas Frame.

2. Glenn W. Most, *The Measures of Praise: Structure and Function in Pindar's Second Pythian and Seventh Nemean Odes* (Göttingen: Vandenhoeck and Ruprecht, 1985), 42.

3. "Sarah Stein's Notes, 1908," ch. 4 in *Matisse on Art*, ed. Jack Flam (New York: Phaidon, 1973).

4. Henri Matisse, "Notes d'un peintre," *La Grande Revue* 52, no. 24 (December 25, 1908). I am grateful to Christopher Green for illuminating this for me and for giving me these references to Matisse.

5. Christopher Green, ed., *Art Made Modern: Roger Fry's Vision of Art* (London: Courtauld Gallery, Courtauld Institute of Art, in association with Merrell Holberton, 1999).

6. Mary Douglas, "Rightness of Categories," in *How Classification Works: Nelson Goodman among the Social Sciences*, ed. Mary Douglas and David Hull (Edinburgh: Edinburgh University Press, 1992), 239–69.

7. Nelson Goodman, *Languages of Art: An Approach to a Theory of Symbols*, 2nd ed. (Indianapolis: Hackett, 1976).

8. Wittgenstein, *Lectures and Conversations on Aesthetics, Psychology, and Religious Belief*, Cyril Barrett, ed. (Oxford: Blackwell, 1966), 5.

9. Quotes from Goodman, *Languages of Art*, 252. "A symbol is the more replete according as proportionately more of its features are functioning symbolically. For instance, in a linear diagram, only differences in position between points on the line, with respect to the coordinates, are significant; the thickness and color of the line do not matter. But in a line drawing—a linear depiction—all these and other features are significant. The drawing is more replete than the diagram," Nelson Goodman and Catherine Z. Elgin, *Reconceptions in Philosophy and Other Arts and Sciences* (Indianapolis: Hackett, 1988), 123.

10. This is part of his distinction between analog and digital systems. Analog systems are "dense" in the sense that the units of which they are made are not, like alphabets or thermometers, finely differentiated, whereas the

units in digital systems have to be strictly differentiated. There is no sense in which they can be replete because they are constructed for purposes that focus only on certain limited properties.

11. This is an oblique reference to T. S. Eliot's theory of the classic, as discussed in Frank Kermode, *The Classic: Literary Images of Permanence and Change* (Cambridge, Mass.: Harvard University Press, 1983).

12. Graeme Auld, "After Exodus and Before Numbers," in *The Book of Leviticus: Composition and Reception*, ed. Rolf Rendtorf and Robert Kugler (Leiden: Brill, 2003), 41–54.

13. Margaret Church, "The First English Pattern Poems," *PMLA* 61 (1946): 636–50.

14. Alastair Fowler, "Cut without Hands: Herbert's Christian Altar," ch 2 in *Presenting Poetry: Composition, Publication, Reception* ed. Howard Erskine Hill and Richard A. McCabe (Cambridge: Cambridge University Press, 1995), 41–51.

15. Jeremy Adler, "Technopaigneia, Carmina Figurata and Bilder-Reime: Seventeenth-Century Poetry in Historical Perspective." *Comparative Criticism* 4 (1982): 107–47.

16. This literary construction is analyzed in chapters 10 and 11 of Mary Douglas, *Leviticus as Literature* (Oxford: Oxford University Press, 1999).

17. Kermode, *The Classic*, 80.

18. Lawrence Gowing, *Turner: Imagination and Reality* (New York: Museum of Modern Art, 1966), 44–45.

19. I thank William Benzone for this information.

20. T. S. Eliot, "Little Gidding," *The Four Quartets*, 1942, *Collected Poems, 1909–1962* (London: Faber and Faber, 1963), 222.

21. Goodman, *Languages of Art*.

Chapter 11. The Latch: Jakobson's Conundrum

1. See "Jorge Luis Borges" in E. Auerbach, *Mimesis: The Representation of Reality in Western Literature* (Princeton, N.J.: Princeton University Press, 1953), 99, 74.

2. Ibid., 90.

3. Ibid., 82–83.

4. Martin Heinzelmann, *Gregory of Tours: History and Society in the Sixth Century* (Cambridge: Cambridge University Press, 2001), 100.

5. Peter Godman, *Poets and Emperors: Frankish Politics and Carolingian Poetry* (Oxford: Clarendon Press, 1987), 8–9, and Heinzelmann, *Gregory of Tours*.

6. Michael Thompson, *Rubbish Theory: The Creation and Destruction of Value* (Oxford: Oxford University Press, 1979).

7. Jean Starobinski, *Les Mots sous les mots: Les anagrammes de Ferdinand Saussure* (Paris: Gallimard, 1971). Saussure collected an analyzed line from legends, between 1905 and 1909, a long exercise on the nature of identity.

8. David Damrosch, *The Narrative Covenant: Transformations of Genre in the Growth of Biblical Literature* (San Francisco: Harper and Row, 1987), 12.

9. E. Fishburn, "Jorge Luis Borges," ch. 10 in *Postmodernism: The Key Figures*, ed. Hans Bertens and Joseph Natoli (Malden, Mass.: Blackwell, 2002), 99, 74.

10. B. Herrnstein Smith, *Poetic Closure: A Study of How Poems End* (Chicago: University of Chicago Press, 1968), 234–60, 237.

11. Ibid., 241.

12. Fishburn, "Jorge Luis Borges," 57.

13. Smith, *Poetic Closure*, 240–41.

14. Ibid.

15. Aaron Wildavsky, Michael Thompson, and Richard Ellis, *Cultural Theory* (Boulder, Colo.: Westview Press, 1990).

16. Cultural theory: This contrast is analyzed in a big literature that at the latest review counted more than seven hundred titles.

17. Katrina C. D. McLeod, "The Political Culture of Warring States China," in *Essays in the Sociology of Perception*, ed. Mary Douglas (Boston: Routledge, 1982), 140–57.

18. *The Analects of Confucius*, trans. Arthur Waley (London: Allen & Unwin, 1964), 21–22.

INDEX

Aaron, 45–46, 49, 60–63, 66, 69,
151*n*6; sons of, 62, 63, 67, 154*n*3
The ABC Murders (Christie), 75–76
Abraham, 152*n*14; and Isaac, 18–
26, 34, 37, 58, 115
Adam and Eve, 14–16, 58
Adler, Jeremy, xii
Adultery, 49, 53–54, 68
Aeneid (Virgil), 116, 117, 118
Alter, Robert, 10
Alternation principle: in *Aeneid*,
116, 117, 118; in book of Numbers, 37, 43–57, 59, 85, 116,
118; in detective fiction, 116; in
epic form, 116; in *Iliad*, 37, 85,
105, 117–24; in large-scale ring
compositions, 116; in Latin
dirges, 116; in ring composition
generally, 37, 116
Analog versus digital systems,
157–58*n*10
Analogies: in book of Leviticus,
133–34; and parallelism, 14, 56;
ring composition as double
sequence of analogies, 34; and
satire, 59; in *Tristram Shandy*,
81–82, 96; as wild and willful, 13
Ancient ring compositions, xi, 1–
16, 28, 38. *See also* Bible; *Iliad*
(Homer); Numbers, Book of;
and other books of the Bible
Antithetic parallelism, 3–4
Apter, David, ix–x

Art, 127–29, 135–38, 142–43,
145, 146
Assyria, 64
Auerbach, Erich, 24, 139–42
Auld, Graeme, xi, 70–71

Balaam, 37, 46, 54
Behl, Aditya, xii
Bible: chiastic structure of, xi, 2, 3,
33, 87; creation story and Garden of Eden in, 14–16, 18, 58;
dating of writings of, xi; and hermeneutic relativism, 144; Isaac
and Abraham in, 18–26, 34, 37,
58, 115; misunderstanding of literary structure of, 10–11; New
Testament of, 33; parallelism in,
2, 3–4, 10, 12, 33; poetry of, x,
3–4, 10; ring composition in, x–
xi, xiii, xiv, 19–26, 152*n*14. *See
also* Genesis, Book of; Moses;
Numbers, Book of; and other
books of the Bible
Bligh, John, 33
Borges, Jorge Luis, 144–45
Borneo, 5
Brain and parallelism, 4–6, 40, 72,
74, 79, 88, 99–100
Brock, Sebastian, 19–20
Burmese, 5

Canaan, 64, 66, 67
Cassuto, Umberto, 14, 33